W0009100
Sachs & VIØLENS

IDW

Become our fan on Facebook facebook.com/idwpublishing
Follow us on Twitter @idwpublishing
Subscribe to us on YouTube youtube.com/idwpublishing
See what's new on Tumblr tumblr.idwpublishing.com
Check us out on Instagram instagram.com/idwpublsing

ISBN: 978-1-63140-774-1 19 18 17 16 1 2 3 4

SACHS & VIOLENS. NOVEMBER 2016. FIRST PRINTING. IDW Publishing, a division of Idea and Design Works, LLC. Editorial offices: 2765 Truxtun Road, San Diego, CA 92106.

Originally published by Marvel as SACHS & VIOLENS issues #1–4.

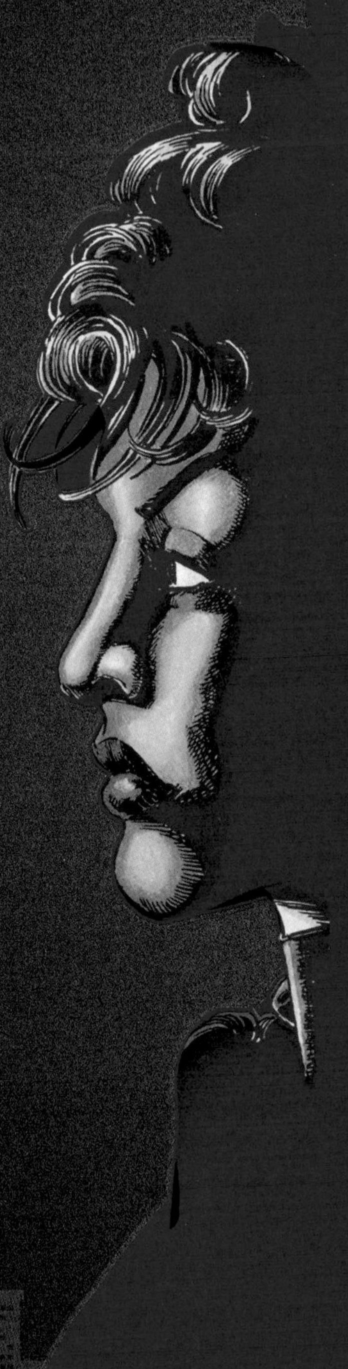

Written by **Peter David**

Art by **George Pérez**

Inks by **George Pérez, Arne Starr**, and **Art Nicholls**

Colors by **John Stracuzzi, Martin Thomas**, and **Tom Smith**

Letters by **John Workman**

Cover Art by George Pérez

Cover Colors by Nelson Dániel

Collection Edits by Justin Eisinger and Alonzo Simon

Collection Design by Ron Estevez

Publisher: Ted Adams

Created by Peter David and George Pérez

Sachs &
VIOLENS
™

CLIK
CLIK
CLIK
CLIK
CLIK

CLIK
CLIK
CLIK
CLIK

CLIK
CLIK
CLIK CLIK CLIK CLIK CLIK CLIK
CLIK
CLIK
CUT!

CUT!
I AM NOT HAPPY, PEOPLE!
SEE THIS FACE? THIS IS THE FACE OF NOT HAPPINESS!
I HAD THOUGHT I WAS GIVING YOU WHAT YOU WANTED, MAURICE. I THOUGHT WE AGREED I SHOULD NOT BE TOO OVER THE TOP. THAT QUIET MENACE FOR THE AXECUTIONER WAS...
OH, ABSOLUTELY, WENDELL. YOU WERE LOCKED IN. HOT. NO PROBLEMS WITH YOU.
WELL, I ASS-UUUME YOU DIDN'T HAVE A PROBLEM WITH ME.
YEAH, WELL, YOU ASS-UUUME WRONG, HART.
FIRST OFF, YOU WERE AS ENTHUSIASTIC AS A DEAD FISH.
THIS GORGEOUS GIRL IS COMING ON TO YOU, AND YOU WERE JUST STARING AT HER! YOU SHOULD LOOK LIKE YOU GOT MAJOR WOOD! INSTEAD, YOU JUST LOOK WOODEN!
AND JESUS, HART! TO TOP IT OFF, YOU LOOKED STRAIGHT INTO THE LENS WHEN THE AXECUTIONER WAS MAKING HIS SWING! AND YOU LOOKED BORED!
IN ANSWER TO YOUR FIRST COMPLAINT: I'D HAVE NO TROUBLE MAINTAINING A LARGE PRICK...
...IF MY DIRECTOR WEREN'T SUCH A LITTLE ONE.
WHAT'D YOU DO, SEND IT INTO THE NEXT COUNTY?!
OH, DEAR. I WAS SO TRYING TO BE RESTRAINED.

AS FOR YOUR SECOND COMPLAINT, I CAN HARDLY BE RESPONSIBLE FOR WHERE YOU CHOOSE TO PLACE YOUR OBNOXIOUS LITTLE CAMERA, CAN I? ALSO, YOU MIGHT WANT TO CONSIDER GETTING ME A DECENT CO-STAR NEXT TIME... ONE WHOSE TITS AREN'T SAGGING INTO MY FACE.
I'LL BE IN MY DRESSING ROOM.
"IF MY DIRECTOR WASN'T SUCH A LITTLE ONE."
JESUS, WHAT A...
WENDELL... MIND TELLING ME WHAT THE HELL YOU'RE DOING DOWN THERE?
PITCHING IN. I'VE INCONVENIENCED THE CREW.
INCONVENIENCED? HOW DID--
YOU CAN STOP LOOKING! I FOUND IT! IT WAS WEDGED UNDER THE OTTOMAN!
DON'T MOVE!
DON'T BUDGE AN INCH! I DON'T WANT TO LOSE THAT EXPRESSION!
PERFECT! WORK WITH ME, BABE! THAT'S IT!
SHOCK! SURPRISE!
CLIK!
WENDY, BABE... THIS IS THE PERFORMANCE OF YOUR LIFE.
AUTO-S
CLIK

FIFTY CENTS, MISTER?
GET OUT OF MY WAY!
GODDAMN TAXIS!
CHECK IT OUT! CHECK IT OUT!
HOW DO I GET TO CARNEGIE HALL?
HON, IT'S JUST NOT WORKING ANYMORE.
GET THE HELL OUT OF MY FACE.
CHECK IT OUT!
GODDAMN TRAFFIC!
A BUCK, MISTER?
MOVE IT ALONG. COME ON.
DIETZ! WHERE HAVE YOU BEEN?!
I SAID THE WEST SIDE OF TIMES SQUARE, BILLY!
I'VE BEEN STANDING AROUND FOR HALF AN HOUR!
GODDAMN HOOKERS!
AND HE NEVER CALLED. THE BASTARD JUST NEVER CALLED...
EXCUSE ME. ARE YOU AN ACTRESS?
BUCK AND A HALF, MISTER?
AW, SHIT!
GODDAMN CITY!
NOW SHOWING!
XXX FEATURE
US ARMED FORCES
ADULT SHOW 24 HOURS
HOURLY RATES AVAILABLE
HEY! MY EYES ARE UP THERE
HEY! CONCHITA!
YEAH! YOU, BABE. SHOW ME WHAT'CHA GOT, CONCHITA.
JUANITA, ACTUALLY. JUANITA JEAN. J.J., TO MY FRIENDS. WHICH YOU'RE NOT.

HEY!!!
CRAZY BITCH!
UNNHH!
ACCKKK!
...

SINGLE
GIRL

I'M SORRY
I'M SORRY
I'M SORRY
THE TRAIN WAS STRUCK.
MY GRAND-MOTHER DIED.
THE DOG ATE MY HOME-WORK.
UH HUH.
YOU LEFT OUT THAT YOU GOT **MUGGED.**

WOW! HOW'D YOU KNOW?
IS THIS THE NEW ISSUE, WITH THE **ORGY** YOU SHOT LAST APRIL?
YEAH. HOW'D I KNOW **WHAT,** J. J.?

THAT I GOT MUGGED.
I WAS **KIDDING.**
WHERE AM I IN THIS...?

OH, WAIT! **HERE** I AM!
SERIOUSLY. **DID** YOU GET MUGGED?

IT WAS MORE SERIOUS FOR **HIM** THAN IT WAS FOR **ME.** I KINDA BEAT THE **SHIT** OUT OF HIM.

JESUS! ARE YOU **OKAY?**
SURE.
WHY DIDN'T YOU **TELL** ME SOME CREEP ATTACKED YOU IN THE **FIRST** PLACE?

I DIDN'T THINK YOU'D **BELIEVE** IT. WHO'D WANNA ATTACK **ME?**

SO WHAT'D THE COPS SAY?
WHAT COPS?
WHAT? DIDN'T YOU SIGN A FORMAL COMPLAINT AGAINST HIM?
HEY, HE ATTACKED ME, I CLOBBERED HIM. ASIDE FROM A BUSTED NAIL, WHAT'S TO COMPLAIN?
J.J., FOR CRYIN' OUT LOUD! YOU JUST LEFT THE GUY BLEEDING SOMEWHERE? YOU DIDN'T EVEN TELL THE COPS?
AND SPEND HOURS COOPED UP IN SOME CRUMMY PRECINCT HOUSE? FORGET IT, ERNIE.
LIFE'S TOO SHORT.

NOW SHOWING
Y'KNOW, J.J., **PART** OF ME WISHES THAT, SOONER OR LATER, YOU'D GET A LITTLE MORE RESPON-SIBLE. YOU KNOW... GROW UP.
GEEZ, ERNIE, YOU SOUND LIKE MY **FATHER**.
YEAH, WELL, **ANOTHER** PART OF ME ADMITS THAT I LIKE YOU **JUST** THE WAY YOU ARE.
OOOH. I WONDER WHAT PART **THAT** IS.

LOOK, I WORRY ABOUT YOU, J.J. ESPECIALLY WITH THESE DISAPPEARING MODELS YOU READ ABOUT. IT'S UP TO FOUR, SO FAR...
I CAN TAKE CARE OF MYSELF, ERNIE. BUT YOU'RE SWEET TO BE WORRIED.
YEAH, SWEET.
JESUS, IT'S 8AM. I FEEL LIKE WE JUST GOT STARTED.
BUY YOU SOME BREAKFAST?
CAN'T. GOT A DATE WITH MY SISTER.
SOME OTHER TIME, HUH?
SURE.
BREAKFAST. DINNER.
GREAT SEX. WHATEVER. JUST SAY THE WORD.

DID YOU SAY SOMETHING, ERNIE?
NAH. JUST THINKING OUT LOUD.

LATER, THEN.
HI.
HI.

ERNIE! GEEZ, TAKE ENOUGH SHOTS OF HER? C'MON, GUY. WHY NOT STOP ADMIR-ING FROM AFAR AND...
WHATTYA WANT, BERT?

WHAT, AN AGENT ISN'T SUPPOSED TO TALK TO HIS CLIENT?
DARK
IF THIS IS ABOUT THE KRAUSS PUBLISHING OFFER...

WELL, OF COURSE IT IS, ERNIE! WHY SHOULD ALL THOSE DYNAMITE WARTIME PICTURES YOU TOOK LANGUISH...

...WHILE YOU DIDDLE AROUND DOING GIRLIE SHOTS? YOU'RE A NEWS PHOTOG, ERNIE.

'BOUT TIME YOU STARTED ACTING LIKE ONE AGAIN.

I'VE BEEN GOING OVER SOME OF YOUR OLD STUFF. THE POWER, THE PERSPECTIVE...
THE UNFORGETTABLE PIZZAZZ OF ERNIE SCHULTZ, CRACK PHOTO JOURNALIST. GEEZ, LOOK AT THIS ONE.

THEY WANT TO OFFER YOU SERIOUS BUCKS, ERNIE. WHO CAN BLAME 'EM? MADONNA WORE OUT INTEREST IN SEX PICTURES.
BUT WAR? VIOLENCE? THAT'S HAPPENING! THAT'S NOW!
OKAY, OKAY ...THINK OF IT AS HUMANITARIAN. PEOPLE SHOULD BE REMINDED OF WHAT WENT ON IN 'NAM, AND...
THAT PICTURE...
WHERE DID YOU GET THAT PICTURE?!
HUH?!
IT WAS IN THE FILES!
WHAT'RE YOU... CRAZY?!
DID YOU EVER THINK, BERT...
...THAT MAYBE SOME OF US WANNA FORGET WHAT HAPPENED OVER THERE?!

HUMANITARIAN, MY ASS! YOU JUST WANNA MAKE A BUCK OFF HUMAN MISERY, YOU BASTARD!
YOU...
YOU...
...URKH...
OH, JEEZ.
BERT ...UH...
YOU OKAY ?
BERT...? I'M SORR--
KEEP THE HELL AWAY FROM ME, SCHULTZ!
GET ANOTHER AGENT! WE'RE FINISHED!
FINE, BERT. WE'RE FINISHED!
SOME THINGS, THOUGH...
...THEY'RE NEVER FINISHED. THEY NEVER END.
NO MATTER HOW MUCH WE'D LIKE 'EM TO.

JEEZ, LOOK AT THOSE **TITS.**

DID'JA **SEE** THESE TITS? I CAN'T **BELIEVE** IT.

SHUT UP, LANE.

STOP WAVIN' IT IN MY FACE.

BUT CAN YOU BELIEVE SHE HAD **TITS** LIKE THIS, TODDY?

AHHH! WATCH OUT!
ARRHHHH!
YOU... MORON!
ME?! I TOLD YOU NOT TO WAVE THAT CRAP IN MY...
OH. SHIT!

HAH!

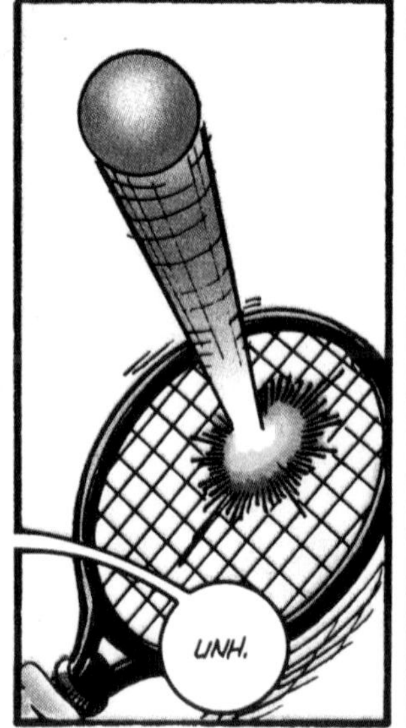
UNH.

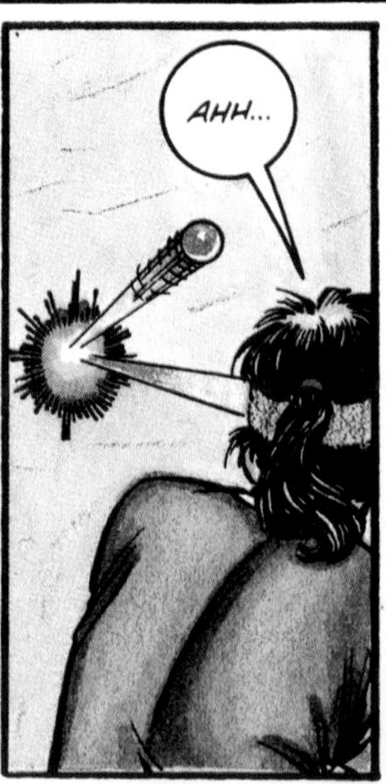
AHH...

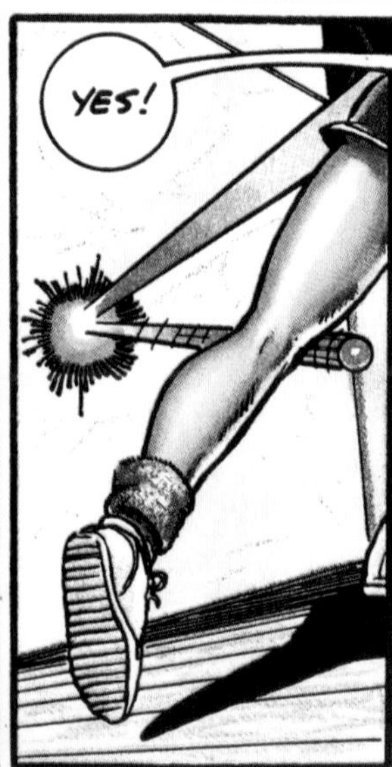
YES!

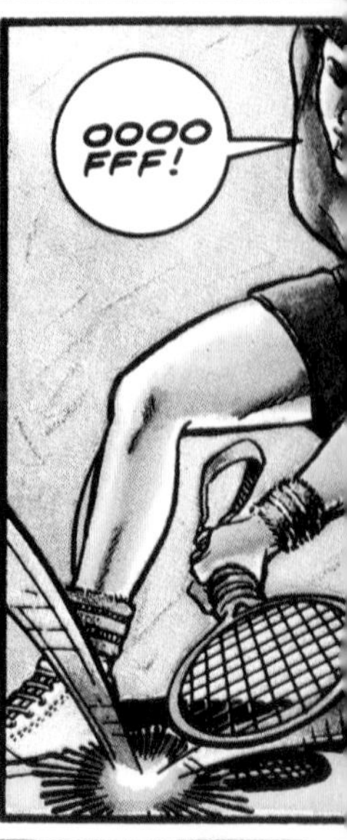
OOOO FFF!

...HUHH...
...HUHH...
LUCKY FOR YOU ...I DON'T PLAY TO WIN.
OH, CHRI--
OH, SURE. SURE YOU DON'T.
I HEARD FROM DAD, BY THE WAY. SOME GIRLIE MAGAZINE WITH YOU IN IT IS ALL OVER THE BASE. HE'S NOT REAL HAPPY.
YEAH, WELL IT PAID OFF VISA, SO IT MADE ME REAL HAPPY.

J.J. ...THE POSING YOU DO ...DO YOU DO IT BECAUSE... Y'KNOW...YOU ENJOY IT? OR IS IT JUST TO ANNOY DAD?

AW, C'MON, MAC. DAD WAS GREAT TO US. WHY WOULD I WANT TO ANNOY HIM?

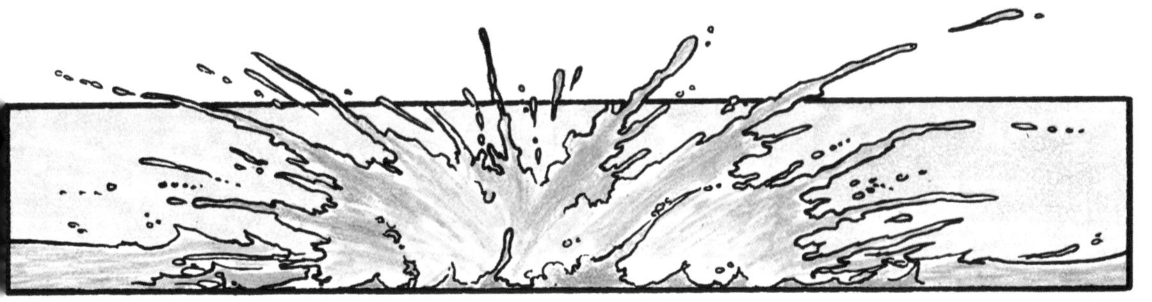

BECAUSE YOU LIKE BEING IN **CONTROL,** J. J.

IT TURNS YOU ON.

OH, LIKE YOU'RE THE ***EXPERT*** ON WHAT TURNS PEOPLE ON.

LOOK, MAC... BEING AN ARMY BRAT WAS A ***FUN*** WAY TO GROW UP. AND DAD TAUGHT US SELF-DEFENSE... THE WHOLE THING.

Y'ASK ME, HE'S JUST ***PISSED*** BECAUSE I DIDN'T PURSUE A MILITARY CAREER.

IT'S ***SO*** UNFAIR! HE DOESN'T BUG ***YOU*** ABOUT ***YOUR*** CAREER CHOICE!

J.J., I ***HARDLY*** THINK IT'S THE SAME THING.

I'M *AFRAID* TO ASK...
DID I SPOT SOME SORT OF BLACK LEATHER OUTFIT IN YOUR BAG?
HEALTH

IT'S FROM *ERNIE'S* COLLECTION. WENDY ASHE, A *FRIEND* OF MINE, IS BORROWING IT.
YOU SPEND SO MUCH *TIME* WITH ERNIE. ARE YOU TWO...?

OH, ERNIE'S A *NICE* OLD GUY, BUT WE'RE JUST...
...friends...

J.J....?
WHAT'S *WRONG?*
'NITA...?

SNUFFED
Final photo session for porno model
stories start on pg. 3

WENDY'S BEEN MURDERED. DE...DE*CAP*ITATED.
MOTHER OF GOD.
NEWS

TAXI! PULL *OVER, RIGHT NOW!*
NEWSPAPERS-MAGAZINES

HEY! THAT WAS *MY* CAB, BITCH!

THE BIG O HAS INFORMED ME THAT HE IS NOT HAPPY. NOT ONE BIT.
Mystery found in val search for driver intensifies
Portrait of death
Do you know this man?
HEY, IT WAS TODD'S FAULT, MAURICE. HE COULDN'T DRIVE FOR--
AWWW, NO. LANE HERE WAS THE ONE WHO SWIPED THOSE PRINTS AND WAS SHOWIN' 'EM TO--
GENTLEMEN, GENTLEMEN...
A DULL ROAR, IF YOU DON'T MIND.
AH! WENDELL! THANKS FOR COMING.
THE PROBLEM IS GENTLEMEN, THAT WE PREFER TO MAINTAIN A LOW PROFILE.
PRIVATE
INSTEAD, THE GIRL'S BODY CAUSED A SCANDAL. PLUS THE PICTURES WEREN'T RETOUCHED YET, SO HART WAS CLEARLY IDENTIFIABLE.
I'M AFRAID, GENTLEMEN, THAT HEADS ARE GOING TO ROLL FOR THIS ONE.
KEEP THE PANIC UP! WORK WITH ME!

YES! A NICE ACTION SHOT!
ALL RIGHT, WENDELL. NOW, I SHOULD THINK.
SPLENDID AS ALWAYS, WENDELL. AND AT LEAST HART FINALLY GAVE A PERFORMANCE WITHOUT TALKING BACK, EH?
I WANT A RAISE.
OUCH, BABE. AS IF I HAVEN'T GOT ENOUGH PROBLEMS.
THINK OF IT AS A TOKEN OF RESPECT.
I HEAR YOU.
big brown

I HEAR YOU, SIR.
NYPD 17TH PCT.
YES, I KNOW THIS KIND OF THING GETS UNWANTED P.R. I--
Lt. E. KELSO HOMICIDE
NO, SIR, I DON'T WANT THIS TO WIND UP AS A TV MOVIE.
NY's FINEST DAD
Lt. ELIOT KELSO
KELSO IN THERE? GOOD!
GOTTA GO, SIR. HOT TIT...UH, TIP... JUST CAME IN.

YOU DETECTIVE SERGEANT KELSO?
I TRIED TO STOP HER, SIR.
AND YOU ARE ...?
PISSED OFF.

YOU'RE HANDLING THE MODELS CASE?
YEAH. YOU GOT A PROBLEM WITH THAT?

WENDY ASHE IS A FRIEND OF MINE. ARE YOU SURE--?

HER PARENTS I.D.'D HER. HERE'S HER HEAD.
WERE THEY RIGHT?
Yeah. Yeah, that's Wendy.

JEEZ...YOU ACTUALLY HAVE SHOTS OF HER GETTING KILLED?
OKAY, LADY, YOU GET BROWNIE POINTS FOR NOT HEAVING.
YOU HEAR OF SNUFF MOVIES? IT'S WHERE--

--WHERE THEY REALLY KILL PEOPLE. I'M NOT STUPID, KELSO.
NO, SWEET-HEART, JUST A BITCH ON WHEELS.
THE NAME'S J. J. SACHS. NOT SWEETHEART.
FINE. SO WHAT WE GOT HERE, MS. SACHS, IS SNUFF PHOTOS. NOW... THE VAN WAS STOLEN, SO THAT WAS A DEAD END. BUT WE'RE TRACKING OTHER LEADS...
BULLSHIT. LIKE WHAT?
LIKE WHY DON'T YOU GET THE HELL OUT OF MY OFFICE UNLESS YOU'VE GOT SOME-THING USEFUL TO SAY?
SCREW YOU.
ALL YOU CIVILIANS THINK THEY KNOW HOW TO DO MY JOB!
WELL, SOMEONE HAS TO.
MOVE.
WOW. AT LAST.
A GIRL I COULD TAKE HOME TO MEET MOM.
ONE WAY

AHHHHHH, Shit, Wend.
THE ART OF
GEORGE PEREZ
NOW AT THE MET
BEEP
HI, J.J.? THIS IS WENDY. JUST CALLING TO RE-MIND YOU TO GET THE BLACK OUTFIT FROM ERNIE.
GOT A SOFT-CORE PHOTO GIG AT SOME PLACE CALLED "SINGLE PICTURES," 216 W. 23RD. IF YOU COULD DROP IT OFF **THERE**, THAT'D BE **GREAT**. I GOTTA **RUN**. DON'T WANNA BE THE LATE WENDY ASHE, Y'KNOW? TAKE CARE.
BEEP
J.J. IT'S ERNIE...

"IF YOU'VE HEARD THE NEWS, THEN CALL ME. IF YOU HAVEN'T, CALL ME BEFORE YOU DO."
RING
YEAH.
I'M DOING IT, ERNIE. I'M GROWING UP. I'M TAKING RESPONSIBILITY.
J.J.! ARE YOU HOME?!
THE GODDAMN PSYCHOS KILLED HER FOR SNUFF PHOTOS, ERNIE.
J. J., FOR GOD'S SAKE, IF YOU KNOW WHERE THEY ARE, CALL THE COPS!
BUT I KNOW WHERE THE STUDIO IS AND I'M GONNA HURT THOSE BASTARDS, ERNIE. MAKE 'EM FEEL WHAT WENDY FELT...
S'LONG, ERNIE.
clik
J.J.!
AWW, HELL!

HARMONY LOVE TOYS
PERFECT. JUST PERFECT.
FINALLY SHE TAKES MY ADVICE ABOUT SOMETHING...
AND SCREWS IT UP!
WHY CAN'T I GET THROUGH TO HER? I GOTTA START USING SIMPLER WORDS. LIKE...
LOVE TOYS...
J.J. ...YOU MAKE ME HOT.
I CAN'T STOP THINKING ABOUT YOU. AND I GOTTA MAKE SURE YOU'RE OKAY.
THE COPS'LL JUST ARREST THEM. NOT GOOD ENOUGH. NOWHERE NEAR.
I'LL GET 'EM FOR YOU, WENDY. THEY'LL NEVER SEE IT COMING. JUST LIKE YOU DIDN'T. EYE FOR AN EYE, LIKE THE BIBLE.
THEY KILLED MY BEST FRIEND. AND I'M GONNA SHOW 'EM WHAT HAPPENS WHEN YOU PISS OFF JUANITA JEAN--
EVEN IF IT MEANS ACTING LIKE I DID BACK IN NAM... WHEN THEY NICKNAMED ME--

SACHS
VIOLENS

Sachs &
VIOLENS
TM

SAFE SACHS

HMN. NICE LEI.
I WOULDN'T KNOW.
I MEANT THE FLOWERED THINGY, RAMBO.
OH. RIGHT. RIGHT. SO... Y'SEEN HER?

SHE IN SOME KINDA TROUBLE, RAMBO?
NEW! FRUITY-FLAVORED BALL GAGS
TUFF CUFFS
MAYBE. SHE'S GOIN' AFTER SOME PEOPLE SHE SHOULDN'T.
SO I'M CHECKIN' SPECIFIC SEX TOY AND SLEAZE PLACES...
...NO OFFENSE...
NONE TAKEN.
20 COPIES GERALD'S GAME
...TO TRY AND TRACE HER STEPS.
FIGURES SHE'D COME HERE FIRST.
HARMONY LOVE TOYS
OPEN
THEY ALL COME HERE FIRST. AND WHAT'S WITH THE COAT? Y'LOOK LIKE A FLASHER.
IT'S COMFORTABLE.
YEAH, WELL... I REMEMBER HER, AWRIGHT.
CAME IN ALL IN A HURRY. THINK SHE SAID HER NAME WAS GIGI...
GLAD HAND LATEX GLOVES
J.J.
YEAH, THAT'S IT.
SHE WANTED SOME-THING LIKE...
BASTINADO BRAND BULLWHIPS
The Knout with Clout!!
DOMINATRIX X-10
...THIS WHAT YOU LOOKIN' FOR, COOKIE?

IT'S OUR TOP OF THE LINE. OUR "DOMINATRIX X-10" MODEL.

EVER SINCE "BATMAN RETURNS," WE BARELY BEEN ABLE TO KEEP 'EM IN THE STORE.
IT'S ALSO GOOD FOR ANIMAL ACTS.

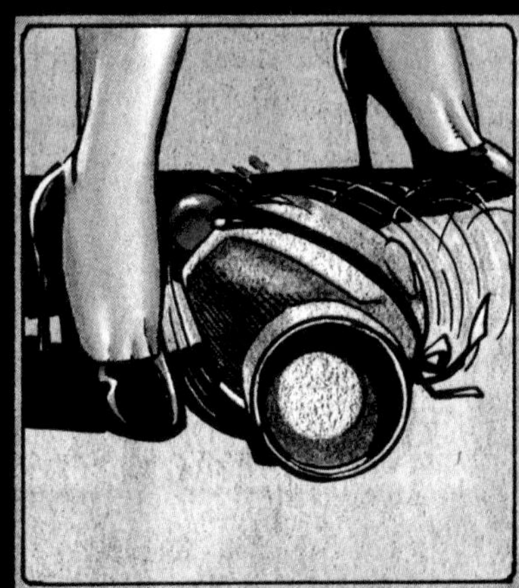

YEAH. I'LL BE USING IT ON ANIMALS.

I TRIED TO GET HER TO TAKE THE WHIP-PLUS-ACCESSORIES PACKAGE, WHICH WE CALL THE "HONEYMOON SURPRISE."
JUST WANTED THE WHIP, THOUGH ...PLUS SOME OTHER ITEMS...

SKIP IT. TELL ME... WHO'S THE TOP DEALER FOR SHIT LIKE, OHHH...

SNUFF MOVIES.
LEMME CHECK MY DIRECTORY.

HMM. HE'S DEAD...
...AND HE WAS ARRESTED...
HERE. TRY GEORGE COMITZ...
RUNS "COMITZ CASTLE" ON 44TH.
HE'S YOUR BEST BET TO...
EH?
YOU COULD'A' SAID "THANK YOU!"
HAVE YOU EVER DONE IT THE TASTY WAY
AND CALL US SOMETIMES, ERNIE! YOUR FATHER AND I WORRY!
SKREEE
"HELLO. OUR LADY OF THE DIVINE WATERS."
"YEAH, HI. I'M TRYING TO REACH MACARTHUR SACHS..."
"I'M SORRY, SIR. YOU MUST HAVE THE WRONG NUM--"
HARMONY LOVE TOYS FOR THE CREATIVE LOVERS
"WAIT, WAIT...UH... SHE'S, UH... SISTER ISABELLA..."
HARMONY LOVE TOYS FOR THE CREATIVE LOVERS
"OH. HOLD ON, SIR."
HARMONY LOVE TOYS FOR THE CREATIVE LOVERS

YEAH. HI. DON'T **TAKE** THIS WRONG, BUT... IS YOUR NAME **MACARTHUR?** AFTER THE GENERAL?

UHM... **YES.** WHO **IS** THIS?
Our Lady of the Divine Water

OH! ERNIE SCHULTZ! **J.J.'S** FRIEND! YES, SHE'S **MENTIONED** YOU.
NO, SHE'S **NOT** HERE. BUT SHE CALLED. SHE WAS **VERY** DISTRAUGHT.

YEAH? WHAT'D SHE **SAY?**

THEY'RE **MONSTERS,** MAC. THEY KILLED WENDY FOR SNUFF PHOTOS. THEY DON'T **DESERVE** TO **LIVE.**

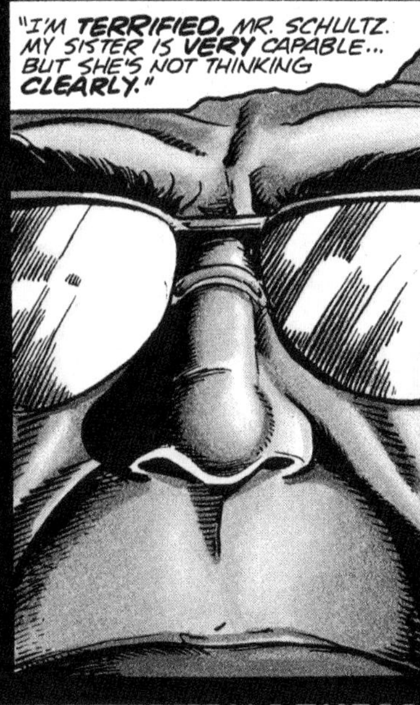
"I'M **TERRIFIED,** MR. SCHULTZ. MY SISTER IS **VERY** CAPABLE... BUT SHE'S NOT THINKING **CLEARLY.**"

"YEAH, WELL, DON'T WORRY. I GOT SOME THOUGHTS ON TRACKING HER DOWN. ALTHOUGH...
VIDEO
BOOKS
ALL NUDE
XXX features KINKY PINKY HIDE & SEKA 3.THE 400 BLOWJOBS
F-STOP
NEW YORK
"...TOSSING A **PRAYER** OR TWO MY WAY COULDN'T **HURT.**"

WELL, WELL... ERNIE SCHULTZ.
HAVEN'T SEEN YOU IN A FEW YEARS... EVER SINCE YOU STORMED OUTTA HERE 'CAUSE I WOULDN'T CARRY...
...YOUR FRICKIN' HIGHBROW PICTURES.
YOU FINALLY WISIN' UP TO WHAT THE MARKET WANTS?
ACTUALLY, GEORGE, YOUR NAME CAME UP A SHORT WHILE AGO.
CHECK THIS.
WHAT'CHA GOT?
AWWW, NO Y' DON'T.
THE COPS HAVE ALREADY BEEN ON THIS FISHIN' EXPEDITION, SCHULTZIE.
THEIR BADGES GOT 'EM SHIT FROM ME, AND YOU GOT NO BADGE.
RALPHIE, SHOW THE MAN OUT.
MAN, YOUR COMIN' IN HERE, THAT TAKES SOME BALLS...
...OH, SHIT...
BREATHE FUNNY, KID, AND I'LL TAKE YOURS.

I REALLY HATE TO SAY IT, GEORGE, BUT I CAN'T RESIST...
UURRKKK!!!
I DON'T NEED NO STINKIN' BADGE.
RALPH! RAL-
SON OF A BITCH!
SON OF A BITCH!
NOW, NOW, RALPH... DON'T BE HASTY.
REMEMBER THE FIRST RULE OF WEAPONRY, NAMELY...
AS SOON AS YOU PULL THE PIN, MR. GRENADE IS NO LONGER YOUR FRIEND.
NOW WHILE YOU PONDER THAT, GO GET GEORGE HERE A PAPER AND PEN SO HE CAN WRITE SOME THINGS HE DIDN'T BOTHER TO TELL THE COPS.

IT'S ABOUT TIME! MAURICE DON'T LIKE T'BE KEPT WAITIN'.
ALL RIGHT, KIDS. GO ON IN.
ARE... ARE WE GOING TO BE ABLE TO GO HOME AFTER THIS?
YES, I PROMISE. STRAIGHT HOME.
Mr. Maurice's Master Studio Authorized Personnel Only
CROSSWORDS
EXCUSE ME.
I'D LIKE TO SEE WHOEVER'S IN CHARGE.
Y'GOT AN APPOINTMENT?
NO.
THEN FERGET IT, DOLL, HE'S TIED UP. WHY DON'TCHA BUZZ OFF FOR TODAY? 'KAY, DOLL?
SIN-GAL MAGAZINE
A SINGLE Publicat

EEEEEEEEEZZZZZT
Mr. Maurice's Master Studio Authorized Personnel Only
Mr. Maurice's Master Studio Authorized Personnel Only
RHODA! WHAT THE HELL IS GOING ON OUT H--?
RHODA'S TIED UP. AREN'T YOU, DOLL?
MMFHFFF!
SO TELL ME... IS IT TRUE THAT THIS IS A GOOD PLACE TO COME FOR...
...HEAD SHOTS?

MAURICE, I THINK WE GOT TROUBLE.
SHE ALONE?
YEAH.
SO WHAT'S THE TROUBLE?
OOO, I LIKE THIS ONE. FIRE. PASSION.
A WOMAN WITH IN-CREDIBLE...
...POSSIBILITIES.
WILL YOU COME IN MY STUDIO?
DEPENDS HOW EXCITED I GET.
HEY, MAURICE! WHAT ABOUT--!
OH, GOD! WHAT WAS I THINKING?
SMILE, RHODA!
clik clik
clik
clik
clikclik
SOMETHING WRONG, BABE?
NO.
NO, IT'S WHAT I... PICTURED.

WE'RE A SMALL OPERATION, BUT WE'RE GROWING. OH, WE'RE DEFINITELY GROWING.
MAY I ASK HOW YOU HEARD OF US?
GOOD NEWS TRAVELS.
FUNNY GIRL. SHE'S A FUNNY GIRL, AIN'T SHE, MAURICE?
OH, QUITE SO. QUITE SO.
I TAKE PRIDE IN MY WORK. AS YOU SEE, WE SPARE NO EXPENSE ...WITHIN OUR BUDGET, OF COURSE.
I'M METICULOUS ABOUT LIGHTING, YOU KNOW. IT'S ALL IN THE LIGHTING, DON'T YOU AGREE ...UHM...?
J.J.
J.J., ARE YOU ALL RIGHT?

J.J., I THINK THERE'S SOMETHING ON YOUR MIND THAT YOU'RE NOT SHARING WITH US.
OH, YEAH?
LIKE WHAT?
OH, LIKE... I DON'T KNOW... THIS PICTURE, PERHAPS.
A PREVIOUS MODEL OF OURS, WENDY, CARRIED IT IN HER HANDBAG, BUT THEN...
YOU KNEW SHE WORKED FOR US, OF COURSE.
YEAH, YEAH, AND I KNOW WHAT YOU BASTARDS ARE.
BASTARDS, YES, BUT STUPID, NO.
YOU, MY DEAR, ARE ABOUT TO BE THE FIRST SUBJECT OF A GANG SNUFF. THE CREW VOLUNTEERED THEIR TIME SINCE THEY'RE SO DEDICATED.
NOW WORK WITH ME ON THIS, ALL RI--?
WE WANNA GO HOME!

SORRY, MAURICE! THEY BUSTED THE LOCK ON THE DRESSING ROOM!
MOMMY! MOMMEE!
PRICK UP YOUR REAR SET #8
JOSEF, PLEASE! I'M IN A SHOOT! GO GIVE THEM SOME CHILDREN'S VALIUM AND STOW THEM UNTIL THE HUNGRY WITCH ARRIVES!
EEEEEEEEE
EEYOO WWTCH!
OH, NOW WHAT? HOW AM I SUPPOSED TO WORK WITH THESE DISTRACTIONS?
ARRHH!
DISTRACTIONS? DISTRACTIONS?!?

I GOT YOUR DISTRACTION RIGHT **HERE,** YOU MURDERING **SACK OF SHIT!**
TAKING BEATINGS WITH STOCKS and BONDS
The PRISONER of ZELDA
DOMINUS
YES! **YES!**
WE'VE NEVER **HAD** ONE WHO FOUGHT BACK! I CAN'T **STAND** IT! IT'S **TOO GOOD!**

KIDS! GET OUTTA HERE!
ARR HHHH!
WOW! IT'S A LION TAMER!
BUT WHERE SHOULD WE GO?!
I SAID GO! WHAT'RE YOU, DEAF?!
I DON'T GIVE A DAMN WHERE! NOW GET THE HELL OUT OF MY WAY!

WHAT'S THE MATTER, MAURICE?
SEE SOMETHING THAT MAKES YOU SHUTTER?

LIKE... YOU'RE OUTTA MEN?
AND, OH, DEAR...IS THAT A LEAKY CANTEEN IN YOUR PANTS...

...OR ARE YOU JUST SCARED TO SEE ME?

C'MON, MAURICE!
WORK WITH ME!
AHHHHH HHHHH!

C'MON BACK, ASSHOLE! I'M NOT DONE!
OHGOD OHGOD OHGOD!

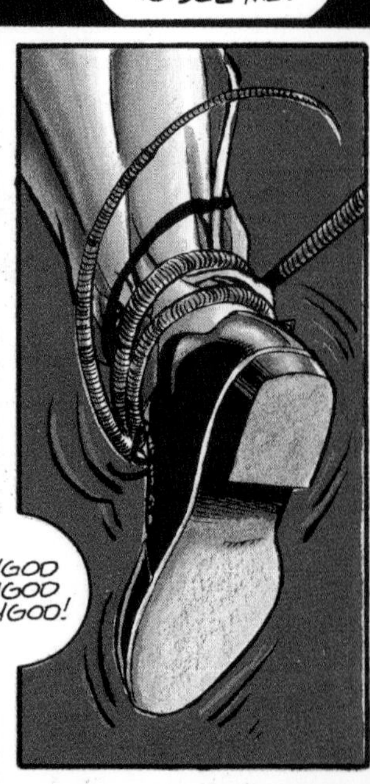

FORGET THAT. IF GOD DIDN'T HELP WENDY, HE SURE WON'T GIVE A SHIT ABOUT YOU!
I'M GONNA MAKE YOU FEEL THE WAY WENDY FELT! I'M GONNA DO YOU LIKE YOU DID HER!
PUSSY WHIPPED

HEY, YOU BRATS! GET BACK HERE!
C'MON, KIDS! I'LL GIVE YOU COOKIES OR SOMETHING!

THAT BITCH SHOULD'VE GOTTEN OUT OF HERE WHILE SHE HAD THE CHANCE!

OKAY, LADY. FUN'S OVER. LET HIM GO.
YOU GOTTA BE KIDDING.

TRY ANYTHING AND I'LL KILL HIM.
FIRST OFF, SWEETHEART, HE'S REPLACEABLE.
SECOND, YOU'VE CONVINCED US YOU'RE GONNA KILL HIM ANYWAY. SO THAT'S A PRETTY EMPTY THREAT.

NOT AS EMPTY AS YOUR HEADS.

YOU GOT 'TIL THREE TO TOSS DOWN THE GUNS.
ONE.
TWO.

OOOFF
THREE.

OKAY, KIDS! YOU'RE FASTER THAN ME! HAPPY?
FIRE EXIT

AND I'VE HAD IT WITH THIS RUNNING CRAP!
FIRE EXIT

UNFF FFFFFF!

WHAT'S THE MATTER? BIG, TOUGH LEATHER LADY FALL DOWN, GO BOOM?
J.J., MY DEAR, I WILL GIVE YOU CREDIT FOR YOUR MAJOR ASSETS.
YOU ARE A FORMIDABLE SCRAPPER. YOU HAVE MORE ENERGY THAN THREE MILE ISLAND. AND YOU'VE GOT A GREAT ASS.
BUT YOUR STRATEGY IS FOR SHIT. YOU NEVER EXPECTED WE'D RECOGNIZE YOU. AND YOU WERE CERTAIN YOUR MORAL OUTRAGE...
...WOULD MAKE YOU INVINCIBLE.
WELL, HECK... LET'S SEE IF YOU'RE RIGHT. J.J., THIS IS THE AXECUTIONER.
HE KILLED YOUR FRIEND.
SIC 'IM.

MILLICENT, IS MY BACK-UP CAMERA LOADED? OH, EXCELLENT!
HEEYAHH!

OOOO OOFFF!
GOOD HEAVENS! J.J., I WAS HOPING FOR MORE THAN THAT!

YOU KNOW...I BET THEY TOLD YOU WENDY DIDN'T SUFFER. THAT SHE FELT NO PAIN.
THEY ALWAYS SAY THAT.

YEEE HAAA!
TAKE IT FROM ME. SHE SUFFERED.

I KNOW, BECAUSE AFTER HER HEAD WAS CUT OFF...
C'MON, MAN, THIS IS RUNNING WAY OVER BUDGET.
FINISH IT.
NO. IT'S OUT OF CHARACTER FOR ME. SHE DESERVES BETTER.
I SAW TEARS DRIBBLING DOWN HER FACE.

IF YOU WOULDN'T MIND SOME CONSTRUCTIVE CRITI-CISM... YOU SHOULD TRY TO **CONTROL** YOUR TEMPER.
MAURICE IS JUST TRYING TO **GOAD** YOU. IT'S MAKING YOU **SLOPPY.** YOUR PERFORMANCE SHOULD BE MORE CONTROLLED--
UNH.
SHUT UP!
SHUT UP, YOU BASTARD! YOU MURDERING BAST--
AHHH! LEGGO MY HAIR!
I'LL **KILL** YOU! PENDEJO PIECE OF SHIT! I'LL **KILL** YOU!
TODAY'S YOUNG PEOPLE. **NO** SENSE OF POETRY.

BEAUTIFUL. **BEAUTIFUL.** SHE'S STILL GOT A LITTLE **FIGHT** IN HER. BUT SHE'S **WOOZY...**

YOU GOT HELPLESSNESS, ANGER...

J.J., SHOW ME A LITTLE **FEAR.** OKAY, BABY? **JUST** A LITTLE...?

SKUH ...**SCREW** YOU.

NEEYA
ARRHHHH

ACCCC CKKKK!
ARHH HGGG GG--!
WHO THE HELL IS THAT?!
WHO THE HELL IS THAT !?!
WHAT IS THIS, A GODDAMN ASYLUM ?!?
J.J.! WHERE ARE YOU?
WHAT'VE YOU BASTARDS DONE WITH HER?
J.J.! ANSWER ME, DAMMIT!
SO HELP ME GOD, IF YOU'VE HURT HER...
J.J.! WHERE ARE Y--

--UUFFF FFFFFFF!

CHRIST, YOU **COULD'VE** SPOKEN UP! WHAT'RE YOU, TAR-FRICKIN'-**ZAN?!**

JEEZ, ERNIE, YOU WERE, LIKE...

I WAS ...**WATCHING** YOU. DIDN'T WANT TO DISTRACT YOUR...YOUR...

THIS ISN'T **FINISHED,** BITCH.

THAT'S **HIM.** THE GUY WHO DID WENDY.

YOU'RE GOING TO HAVE A DEATH **WORTHY** OF OUR ART!
I'LL TAKE YOU **BOTH TOGETHER!**
A **SONATA** OF **SAVAGERY, FIT** FOR WARRIORS SUCH AS OURSELVES! A TRUE, **POETIC CLIMAX!**

ARRHHH!
JESUS, WHAT AN ASSHOLE.

AW, MAN! ERNIE, I COULD'A' TAKEN HIM! WHY'D YOU SHOOT HIM?!
BECAUSE HE WAS TRYING TO KILL YOU.
THEY TRY TO KILL YOU, YOU TRY TO KILL THEM. THAT'S HOW WAR WORKS, SACHS.

YOU'RE AN ARMY BRAT, YOU SHOULD KNOW.
DANCING AROUND IS IDIOTIC. JUST DO IT AND MOVE ON.

HOLD IT. I HEAR SOMETHIN'.

LIKE A MOUSE, MAYBE ...OR...

NO. A RAT.

EXIT

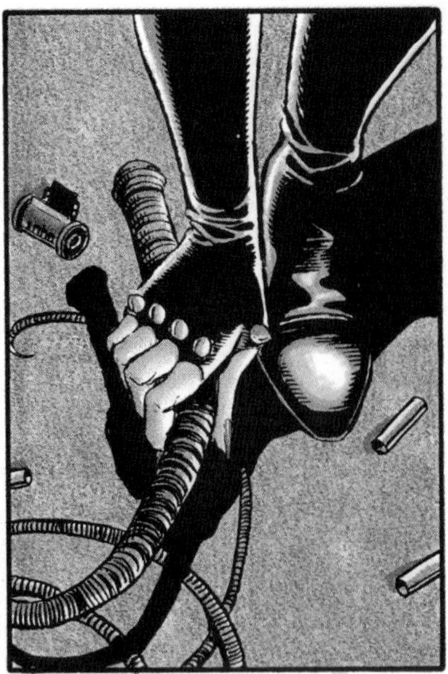

A BIG, ARTSY-FARTSY PICTURE-TAKING RAT.

ACCK KKKK!
OH, NOW I'M PISSED! NOW I AM SO PISSED!
GO AHEAD, BITCH! YOU WANNA DO ME LIKE WE DID YOUR FRIEND? SO DO IT ALREADY!
DO IT!

I...
HE'S HELPLESS. YOU CAN'T KILL HIM IN COLD BLOOD. LEAVE HIM FOR THE COPS.

YEAH. YEAH, I SHOULD'A' KNOWN. THAT'S JUST BEAUTIFUL.
Y'KNOW WHAT'S BEST? I'M GONNA WALK...
...'CAUSE YOU KILLED ALL THE WITNESSES, RIGHT? UNLESS YOU'RE GONNA TESTIFY, HUH?

YOU SCREWED UP! I'M GONNA WALK... AND MY BOSS'LL TAKE YOU DOWN! I'M LOOKIN' AT DEAD PEOPLE! I--

HEY! WH...WHAT'RE YOU DOING?! YOU SAID--!

I SAID SHE SHOULDN'T. ME, I'VE KILLED INNOCENT PEOPLE BEFORE.
OLD HABITS DIE HARD. BUT YOU'LL DIE EASY.
clik

IN OTHER WORDS, SHIT-FOR BRAINS ...IT'S A WRAP.
BLAM!

NEXT SHOT'S IN A GLASS, HUH, ERNIE?
SHUT UP AND MOVE.
WHATEVER YOU SAY, ERNIE. YOU'RE THE BOSS.
BUCKLE YOUR SEAT-BELT.
YOU'RE KIDDING.
IT'S THE LAW. BESIDES, WHY TAKE UNNECESSARY RISKS?
OH, JEEZ, OH, JEEZ, MY HEART'S PUMPING. IT'S LIKE...
GOD, EVERYTHING SEEMS JUMPED UP! AND YOU WERE INCREDIBLE! MAN, WE DID IT! I...
YOU'RE BABBLING, J.J. CALM DOWN.
I DON'T WANNA CALM DOWN. I WANT TO GET MORE EXCITED.
HOW ABOUT WE PULL OVER SOMEWHERE AND SEE HOW EXCITED WE CAN GET.
YEAH, SURE. RIGHT.
I'M SERIOUS, ERNIE.
YEAH?
YEAH.
WELL, I DON'T THINK WE'D WANNA WAKE THE KIDS.
KIDS?! YOU BROUGHT THOSE KIDS ALONG?!
AW, JEEZ, ERNIE...
I COULDN'T JUST LET 'EM WANDER THE STREETS. IT'S A JUNGLE OUT THERE.
YEAH.
TELL ME ABOUT IT.

Sachs & VIOLENS™

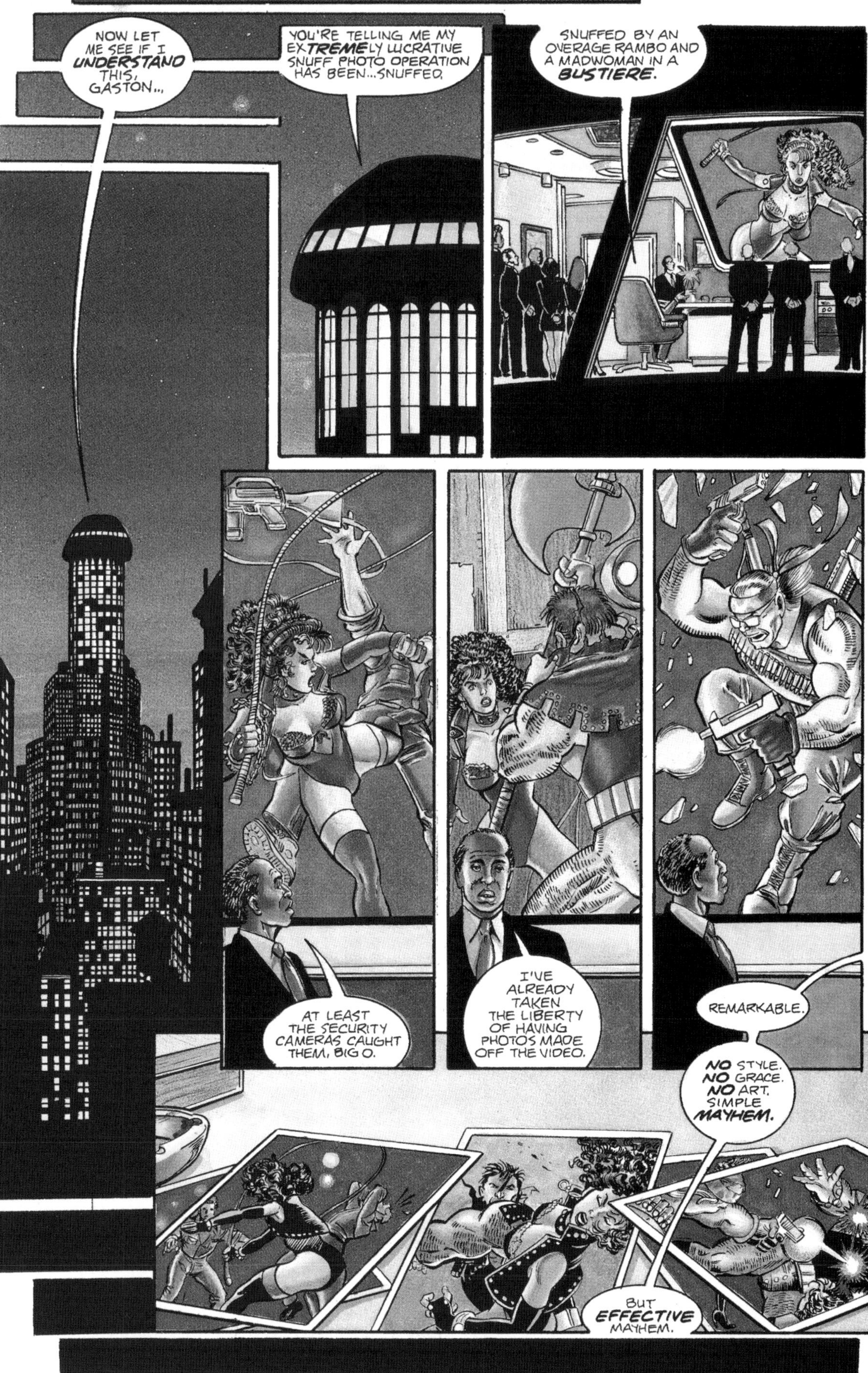
NOW LET ME SEE IF I UNDERSTAND THIS, GASTON...
YOU'RE TELLING ME MY EXTREMELY LUCRATIVE SNUFF PHOTO OPERATION HAS BEEN...SNUFFED.
SNUFFED BY AN OVERAGE RAMBO AND A MADWOMAN IN A BUSTIERE.
AT LEAST THE SECURITY CAMERAS CAUGHT THEM, BIG O.
I'VE ALREADY TAKEN THE LIBERTY OF HAVING PHOTOS MADE OFF THE VIDEO.
REMARKABLE.
NO STYLE. NO GRACE. NO ART. SIMPLE MAYHEM.
BUT EFFECTIVE MAYHEM.

LET ME TAKE THESE PICTURES TO THE COPS. THESE TWO NUTS ARE ALREADY A PAIN IN THE ASS.

LET THE COPS HANDLE THEM. WHAT ELSE ARE WE PAYING BRIBES FOR IF--

GASTON, YOU'RE AN IDIOT.
THE POLICE MIGHT CAPTURE THEM.

WE DON'T WANT THEM CAPTURED... ALIVE... TO SPILL WHATEVER THEY'VE LEARNED ABOUT US.
WE WANT THEM DEAD.

I WANT THEM DEAD.
UNDER-STOOD, GASTON?
YES, BIG O.

OH...AND GASTON...
YES, BIG O?

THAT IS WHAT A GENUINE PAIN IN THE ASS FEELS LIKE.
MAKE SURE TO ELIMINATE THEM BEFORE THEY BECOME GENUINE PAINS-IN-THE-ASS... OR EVEN WORSE...

...BALL-BREAKERS.
Y-YES, BIG O...
DON'T BLEED ON THE CARPET ON THE WAY OUT.

RING! RING! RING!
YEAH.
YEAH? A CALL FROM THE IVORY TOWER.
PUT 'IM ON.
BIG O... TO WHAT DO I OWE THE PLEASURE?
UNH HUNH.
UNH HUNH.
GOT THE KIDS, TOO, HUH?
NO. NO, MOVING THE OPERATION ISN'T NECESSARY. LET 'EM COME. I'LL BE READY.
BIG O SOUNDED NERVOUS. THAT'S A FIRST.
WELL, DON'T WORRY, TEDDY. WE KNOW HOW TO DEAL WITH TROUBLE-MAKERS, DON'T WE?

Sachs and Violens II

KRAK

KRAK

HAIII!

HAIIII!

HAIII--

VIOLENS BEGETS VIOLENCE

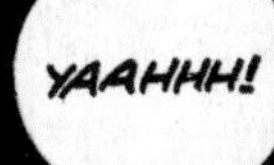

I GOT 'EM, WENDY.
I GOT THE BASTARDS WHO KILLED YOU.
Y'HEAR ME, WENDY?! I GOTTTT 'EM!!!
J.J.? WHAT'RE YOU YELLING ABOUT? YOU OKAY?
HEY! SACHS! STOP SCREWING AROUND. WHERE ARE YOU?
J.J., THIS ISN'T FUNNY!
WE PROBABLY GOT MOB GUYS ON OUR ASS! I'M PARANOID ENOUGH AS IT IS!
SO DON'T GO DIS-APPEARING ON--
--me.

HI.
HI.
I, UH, GOT THE KIDS BEDDED DOWN IN THE CAR. SO I'LL JUST, UH...
COME ON IN, "VIOLENS". THAT IS YOUR OLD NICKNAME, ISN'T IT?
AW, JEEZ, CALL ME ERNIE, OKAY? AND I, UH...DIDN'T BRING A SUIT.
I'VE POSED NAKED FOR YOU ENOUGH TIMES. FAIR'S FAIR.
IT'S COLD.

I'LL HEAT YOU UP.
AWWW, JEEZ...

WHEN WE WERE TAKING ON THOSE GUYS...GOD, IT WAS LIKE NOTHING I EVER FELT BEFORE.
WE COULD'VE BEEN KILLED.
I KNOW. BUT WE SURVIVED. AND NOW I FEEL MORE ALIVE THAN I'VE EVER BEEN.

AND YOU! CHRIST, YOU WERE SO POWERFUL! SO SEXY! I CAN'T BELIEVE IT TOOK ME THIS LONG TO REALIZE...

J.J., I'M OLD ENOUGH TO BE YOUR... YOUR OLDER BROTHER.
I'M SO WIRED UP... LIKE SOME CRAZY HIGH...

YOUR HEART'S POUNDING. SO'S MINE. FEEL IT. FEEL ANYTHING OF MINE YOU WANT...

THIS IS WRONG, OKAY? YOU'RE NOT THINKING CLEARLY.
NO, VIOLENS. I'M THINKING CLEARLY FOR THE FIRST TIME.

IT'S ERNIE, OKAY? ERNIE SCHULTZ! VIOLENS WAS A LONG TIME AGO!
AND I... UH...

LOOK... ONE OF US IS GOING TO HAVE TO... UH...
I'M JUST GONNA, UH... GO NOW...SO YOU CAN, UH...

GEEZ, WHAT AM I... NUTS?!

YOU WIN! OKAY?! YOU W--
--OOAA AHHHHH!

AHHHH! SHIT!

IT'S FREEZING IN HERE, YOU CRAZY BITCH!!!
DON'T WORRY.

BECAUSE WE ARE GONNA BOIL OFF--

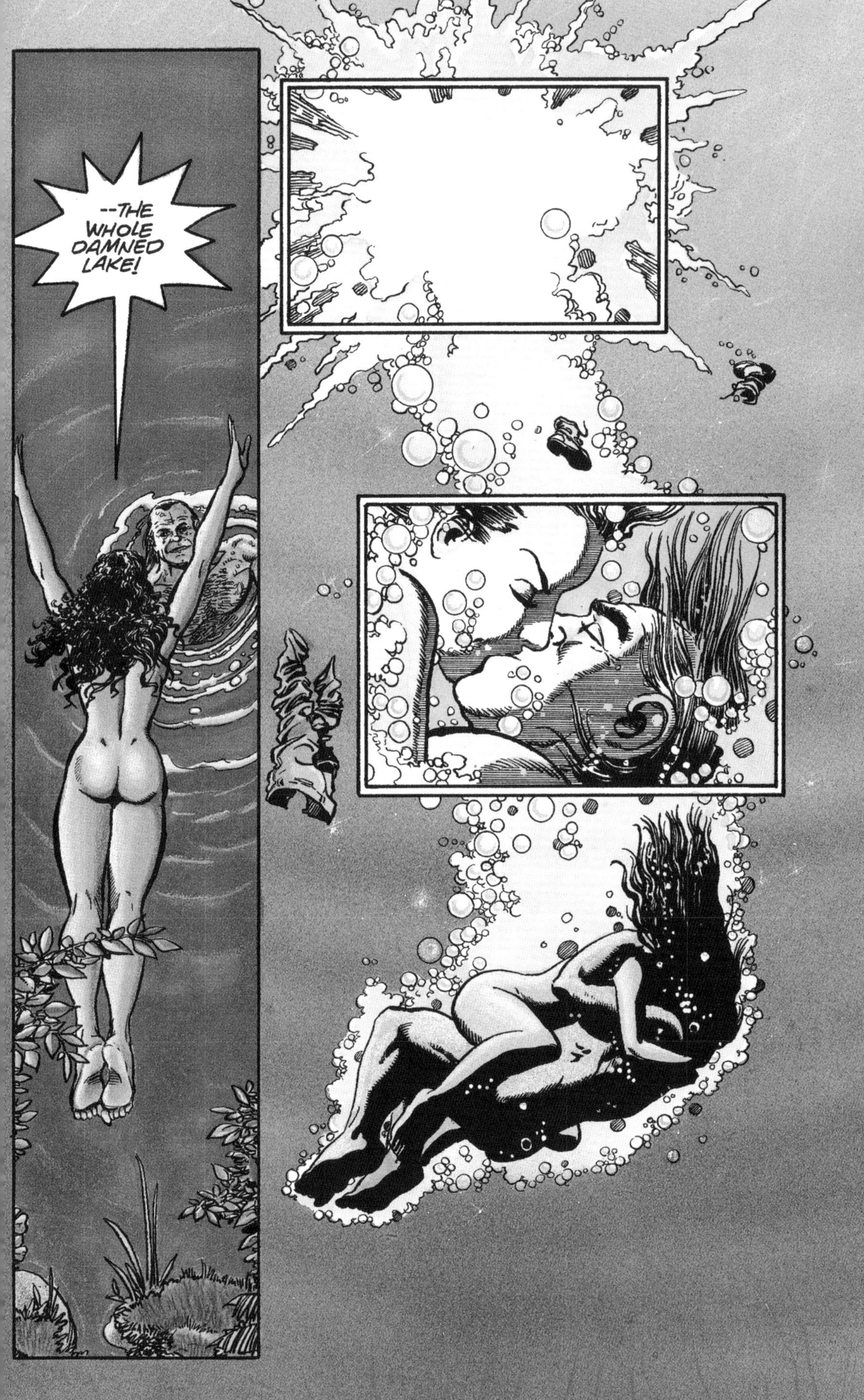
--THE WHOLE DAMNED LAKE!

SUNSHINE
EDUCATIONAL
PRODUCTS
QUIET. HE MIGHT HEAR YOU.
TAXI
GERRY GOOP MODELING CLAY
LET 'IM. I DON'T GIVE A DAMN ANYM--
HEY, KIDS! HUG-A-MUGGER! I'M BACK!
YOUR OLD PAL... GERRY THE GERRY-MANDER!
GERR LUVS
SMILE!
AND WE'RE GONNA HAVE SOME HUG-A-MUGGER FUN!
HOW ARE GERRY'S KIDS, HUH ?!?
GUESS WHAT, KIDS! IT'S TIME FOR ONE OF YOU TO GO TO THE LAND OF EYE-MAGINATION! WHO WANTS TO GO? LET'S SEE HANDS...
...AND I HOPE THEY'RE CLEAN, HEE-YUKK!

WHAT'SA MATTER, KIDS? YOU LOOK SCARED!
J-JACKIE SAYS THAT THE KIDS WHO GO WITH YOU TO EYE-MAGINATION LAND NEVER COME BACK.
GERRY LUVS U

SO?
JACKIE... DID'JA EVER THINK MAYBE THEY'RE HAVING SUCH A GOOD TIME, THEY DON'T WANNA BACK COME BACK?

I THINK THEY... THEY CAN'T COME BACK. THAT YOU DO BAD THINGS TO THEM.
I ♥ GERRY

I THINK YOU'RE NOT OUR FRIEND AT ALL.

WELL, HUG-A-MUGGER, JACKIE! THAT'S HOW MUCH YOU KNOW!
I GUESS I'LL JUST HAVE TO SHOW YOU MYSELF!

KIDS! SING OUR SONG TO JACKIE! IT'S JUST LIKE "TWINKLE TWINKLE," REMEMBER!

WELL?!? SING!!!

WE LOVE GERRY, YES SIREE
HE'S THE ONE FOR YOU AND ME

MOUTH SO BIG AND TAIL SO GRAND
TAKES US TO HIS MAGIC LAND

AND IF YOU ARE LUCKY, TOO
SOMEDAY HE MIGHT COME FOR YOU

CHOMP!

'BYE, KIDS! SEE YA NEXT TIME!
C'MON, JACKIE! WE'RE GONNA HAVE HUG-A-MUGGER FUN!

-:SNIFF:-
JEEZ, IT'S LIKE HAVING A PLAY-GROUND IN JURASSIC PARK...

I THINK THEY WERE **DOING** IT.

DOING **WHAT?**

IT. YOU KNOW...THE THING YOUR MOM AND DAD DID TO GET YOU.

MY MOM SAID SHE GOT ME FROM A MACHINE IN A LADY'S ROOM.

I'M... NOT SURE WHAT CAME OVER ME LAST NIGHT.

WHAT CAME OVER YOU? J.J., IT WAS INCREDIBLE! YOU WERE...

I WASN'T MYSELF, OKAY? LET'S JUST... JUST REMEMBER IT WAS GREAT AND LEAVE IT AT THAT, HUH, ERNIE?

SURE.
WHAT-EVER YOU SAY.

SHORTLY...
SO YOU REALLY THINK IT'S NOT SAFE TO GO HOME?
NOT UNTIL WE READ SOME NEWS REPORTS. SEE WHAT THE COPS ARE SAYING.
BEST THING TO DO RIGHT NOW IS DROP THE KIDS OFF WITH SOME LOCAL COPS... IF I CAN TELL FROM THIS MAP WHERE IN JERSEY WE ARE...

WE'RE HERE.
AND OUR FRIENDS... OTHER KIDS, TRAPPED BY MOLOCH... ARE HERE. YOU TAKE THIS EXIT...

HOW THE HELL ARE YOU SO GOOD WITH MAPS?
"CARMEN SAN DIEGO" IS MY FAVORITE PROGRAM.

MORE IMPRISONED KIDS! ERNIE, THAT SOUNDS EXCITING! MAYBE WE SHOULD CHECK THIS OUT!
CHECK IT OUT?! J.J., WE'RE IN TROUBLE UP TO OUR ASSES ALREADY!

WHAT WE'RE GONNA DO IS BRING THESE KIDS TO THE COPS...
...RRRRRIIGHT AFTER WE CHECK OUT THESE OTHER TRAPPED TYKES.
J.J.! 'NITA, ARE YOU ALL RIGHT?!
I'M FINE, MAC. REALLY.
OUR LADY OF THE DIVINE WATERS ROMAN CATHOLIC SCHOOL
DID YOU SEE THE PAPERS? THE POLICE CAUGHT WENDY'S KILLERS! THERE WAS SOME SORT OF SHOOTOUT!
NO, I HADN'T HEARD. I GOT OUT OF TOWN TO COOL OFF A BIT.
A SHOOT-OUT, HUH? NO SURVIVORS? UH... HOLD ON, SIS.
THE COPS ARE TAKING CREDIT FOR CRACKING THE SIN-GALS CASE.
GOOD.
ME AGAIN. HEY, MAC... THERE'S SOMETHING I WANNA CHECK WITH YOU.
A NAME THAT SOUNDS FAMILIAR ...SPELLED M-O-L-O-K.
M-O-L...OH! THAT'S "CH", NOT "K".
MOLOCH. WAS AN OLD TESTAMENT GOD. LOOKED LIKE A BULL, SACRIFICED CHILDREN. 'NITA... WHY ON EARTH ARE YOU ASKING?

CROSSWORD PUZZLE.
MAC, DON'T **WORRY** ABOUT ME. I'LL BE HOME SOON. I'LL BE FINE.
YEAH... BYE.

I **HATE** LYING TO HER.

WHICH WAS THE LIE? THAT YOU'D BE HOME SOON... OR THAT YOU'LL BE ***FINE?***

THAT NAME THE KIDS MENTIONED... DID IT CHECK OUT?
KINDA. IT'S AN ANCIENT BULL GOD.

STILL THINK IT'S ***BULL,*** FLETCHER?

SO THIS J.J. SACHS WAS A FRIEND OF WENDY ASHE'S. SO ***WHAT,*** KELSO?
WHAT ABOUT THE MARTIAL ARTS TRAINING DUMMY?

SO SHE ***TRAINED.*** BIG DEAL.
A SINGLE GIRL IN NEW YORK. WHY ***NOT?***

JUNK FOOD. I THOUGHT MODELS ATE HEALTHY...!

HEY, KELSO... DIDN'T THE CORONER SAY SOMETHING ABOUT "WHIP MARKS"?
ON SOME OF THE BODIES, *YEAH.*

GUESS WHO PURCHASED A WHIP.
HARMONY LOVE TOYS
AT LAST HE SEES THE LIGHT.

SUNSHINE
EDUCATIONA
PRODUCTS

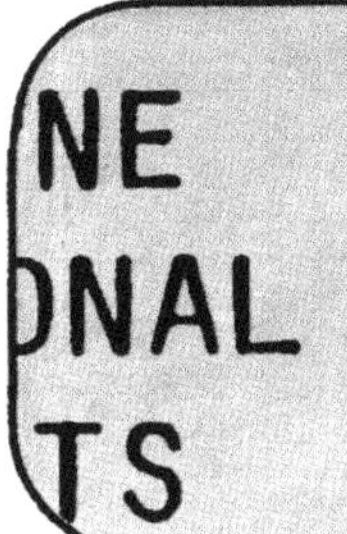
NE
ONAL
TS

CHECK IT OUT, ERNIE. WHY WOULD "SUNSHINE EDUCATIONAL TOYS" HAVE A GUARD ARMED WITH A MACHINE GUN?

DON'T LAUGH. I DID **BABY PICTURES** FOR A WHILE. SOME OF THOSE TODDLERS ARE **VICIOUS.**
GODDAMN, ERNIE, THE BRATS WERE RIGHT.
LET'S GO IN AND BUST THEIR FRIENDS **OUT.**

NO WAY IN HELL.
SUNSHINE EDUCATIONAL PRODUCTS
WE CAN **DO** IT, ERNIE! WE **GOTTA** SEE THIS THROUGH.

C'MON, VIOLENS! WE'RE SO **GREAT** TOGETHER! LIKE AT SIN-GALS, AND THEN BY THE LAKE ...REMEMBER?
J.J., DOES THE PHRASE "**MOOD SWINGS**" MEAN ANYTHING?

PLEASE **DO** SOMETHING, MR. VIOLENS! GET OUR FRIENDS OUT OF THERE!
BEFORE THE DINOSAUR EATS THEM!

DINOSAUR?

C'MON, JACKIE! YOU'RE NOT STILL MAD AT OL' GERRY, ARE YOU? I HOPE-ITTY-HOPE NOT!
ARE... ARE YOU GONNA KILL ME?
NO, SON.
YOU'RE GOING ON A TRIP.
A TRIP TO A BETTER PLACE... TO PEOPLE WHO WILL LOVE YOU.
REMEMBER, YOUR OWN PARENTS DIDN'T REALLY WANT YOU, OR THEY'D HAVE COME FOR YOU BY NOW.
I'LL GET YOU FOR THIS, YOU LYING SHIT-HEADS!
THOSE ARE NOT NICE WORDS, JACKIE! LET'S TEACH YOU NEW WORDS, LIKE:
"WHITE SLAVERY."
PAD-BID
SUNSHINE EDUCATIONAL PRODUCTS
BYE-BYE, JACKIE! HUGS ALL AROUND!

SUNSHINE
EDUCATIONAL
PRODUCTS

HMM?
I THOUGHT THE VAN JUST WENT OUT TEN MINUTES AGO.

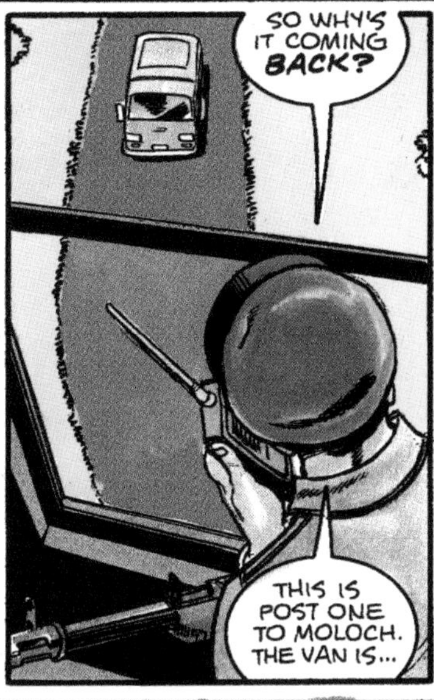
SO WHY'S IT COMING BACK?
THIS IS POST ONE TO MOLOCH. THE VAN IS...

SHIT! THE VAN'S PICKING UP SPEED!
SUNSHINE
EDUCATIONAL
PRODUCTS
THE VAN? WHAT'RE YOU TALKING AB--

MOVE! OUTTA THE WAY!!!
ACCKKK!

THERE WAS NO ONE DRIVING IT!

NO ONE, MY ASS! IT'S A COUPLE OF KIDS!
O...OKAY, YOU GUYS. YOU BETTER LET MY FRIENDS GO.

THE BACK'S EMPTY, MOLOCH.
WELL, WELL. KATIE AND SAMMY, IF I'M NOT MISTAKEN.
SO TELL ME, KIDS...

WHERE THE HELL ARE MY MEN?! AND JACKIE?!
YOU BRATS ARE IN SO MUCH TROUBLE--!

NOT AS MUCH AS YOU'RE IN, YOU FAT DOUCHE-BAG.

DON'T SHOOT!
F-STOP NEW YORK
DON'T SHOOT!

SCREW 'EM! SHOOT!

CRASH

WHAT THE HELL'S GOIN' ON DOWN THERE?
OUNDS LIKE GODDAMN ARZONE!

OOOF FFFF!

MADRE DE DIOS!
NO ME MATA! NO ME MATA!

DON'T KILL ME! JESUS, GOD, DON'T, I...

HOLEEE SHIT...

I... I'M A STRIP-O-GRAM. FOR LARRY.
THE AGENCY... THEY GIMME THIS ADDRESS, I SWEAR...
WE AIN'T GOT NO LARRY HERE, BABE...

BUT DON'T LET THAT STOP YA.
WAIT! MOLOCH SAID SOMETHING ABOUT A BROAD--!

BUDDA! BUDDA! BUDDA!
OOOO OOFF!
-ACKKK-
HEE-YAAHHH!
-ARH HHH-
awgod awgod
KIDS! MOVE YOUR ASSES!
STAY LOW AND GO FOR YOUR FRIENDS, LIKE WE PLANNED!
GREAT. ON TOP OF EVERYTHING ELSE, I'LL GET NAILED FOR CHILD ENDANGERMENT.
I KNEW IT! IT'S THE BITCH FROM NEW YORK!
MICKEY, WAIT!
EEYAA RHHH!

UNN, FFFF!
BUDDA! BUDDA!
SHUKK
KIDS? YOU HERE?
DON'T BE SCARED! IT'S ME, MISTER... VIOLENS!
OKAY, THE MODESTY BLAISE RIFF WORKED!
CAN'T BELIEVE I'M STAYING SO CALM...
HEY!
WHAT?!
YOU UP THERE? I'M COMIN' UP!
JESUS, DON'T SNEAK UP ON ME LIKE THAT!
WHERE'S ERNIE?!
BEHIND US, I GUESS.
THE OTHER KIDS ARE THIS WAY! C'MON!

ARRGH HHHHH!!!
AN OLD MAN! I DON'T BELIEVE IT.
THE BIG O WAS WORRIED ABOUT AN OLD MAN.
UNHHH!
SHUK
OOO OFF!!!
GET BACK HERE!
WHAT'RE YOU, SCARED?
OH, YEAH, FAT MAN.
SHITLESS.
GOOD.
BEING AFRAID IS THE ONLY SMART THING YOU'VE DONE TODAY.

C'MON! MOVE! MOVE!
OOOH, I'M SHAKING.
BUT GERRY'S GONNA BE MAD!
CRIPES, WILL YOU KIDS HAUL ASS!?
I DON'T THINK SHE LIKES KIDS.
WHO GIVES A DAMN!? HURRY!
I ♡ GERRY

IS THAT ALL OF 'EM?
I THINK SO.
GOOD. LET'S...

OOOO OOFF!!!

HUG-A-MUGGER, KIDS.
YOU CAN'T JUST RUN OFF LIKE THAT!
YOU'LL HURT MY FEEEELLINGS!
MEANWHILE...

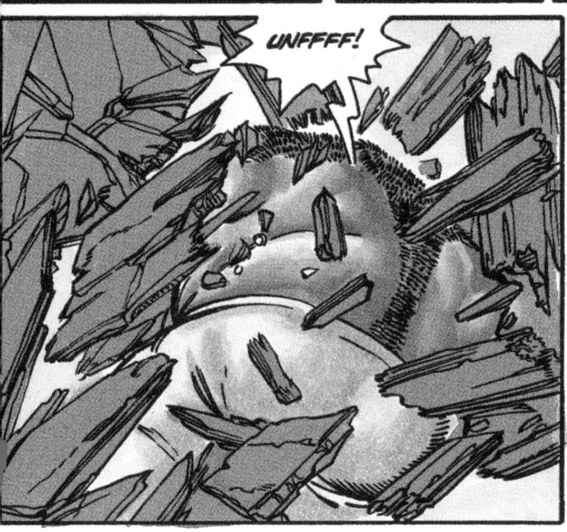
UNFFFF!

C'MON, "VIOLENS," LET'S SEE WHAT YOU'RE MADE OF!
HELL, LET'S DECORATE THE FLOOR WITH IT.

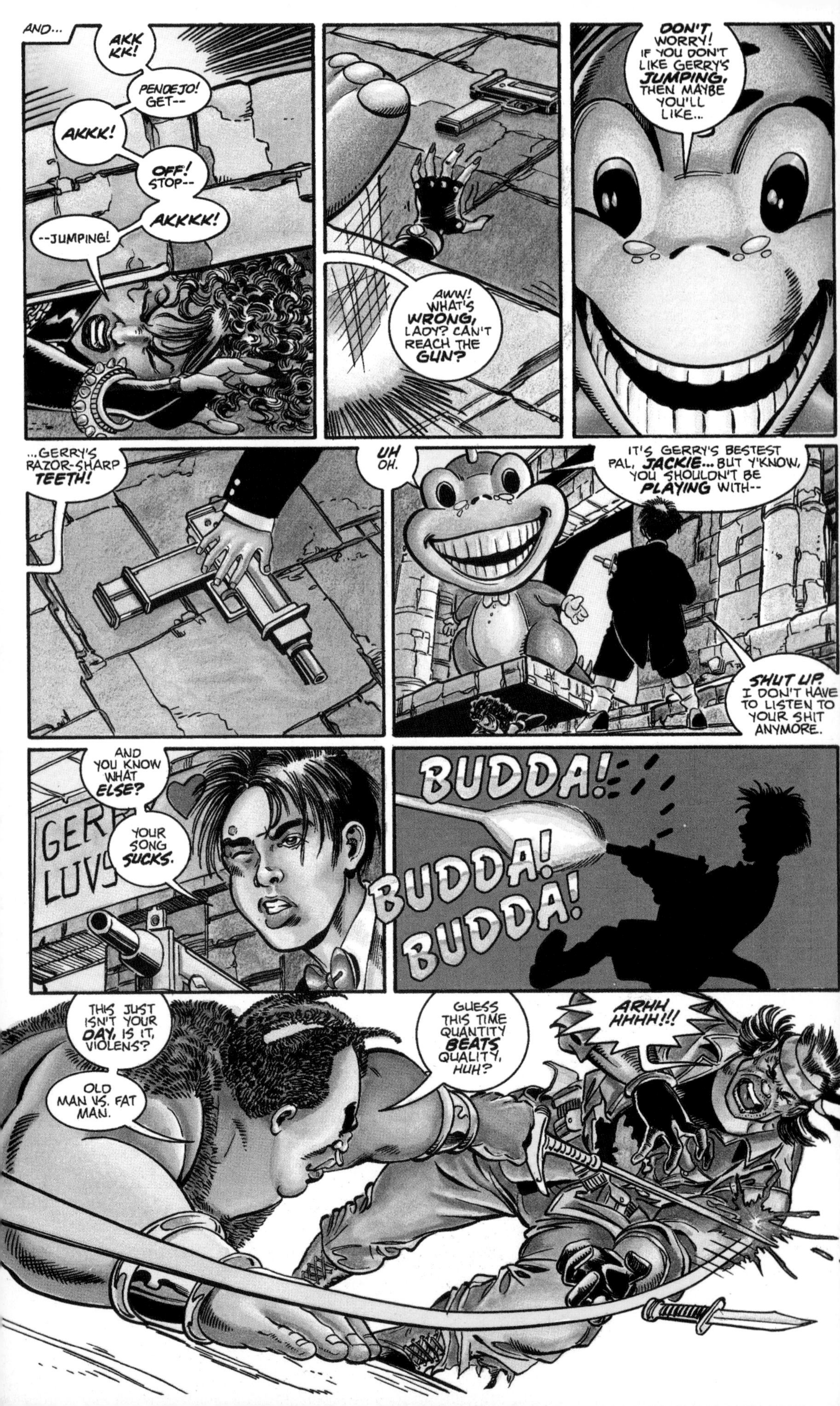
AND...
AKK KK!
PENDEJO! GET--
AKKK!
OFF! STOP--
AKKKK!
--JUMPING!
AWW! WHAT'S WRONG, LADY? CAN'T REACH THE GUN?
DON'T WORRY! IF YOU DON'T LIKE GERRY'S JUMPING, THEN MAYBE YOU'LL LIKE...
...GERRY'S RAZOR-SHARP TEETH!
UH OH.
IT'S GERRY'S BESTEST PAL, JACKIE... BUT Y'KNOW, YOU SHOULDN'T BE PLAYING WITH--
SHUT UP. I DON'T HAVE TO LISTEN TO YOUR SHIT ANYMORE.
AND YOU KNOW WHAT ELSE?
YOUR SONG SUCKS.
GER
LUVS
BUDDA!
BUDDA!
BUDDA!
BUDDA!
THIS JUST ISN'T YOUR DAY, IS IT, VIOLENS?
OLD MAN VS. FAT MAN.
GUESS THIS TIME QUANTITY BEATS QUALITY, HUH?
ARHH HHHH!!!

IS THE BROAD HERE, TOO? THE ONE IN LEATHER?
HOPE SHE GIVES ME MORE OF A FIGHT THAN YOU DID, VIOLENS.
THIS... THIS AIN'T OVER, YOU SON OF A BITCH.
YES IT IS.
HUNH?!
KRAK
UNF FFF!
NO
IT'S
NOT.
CLANGITY CLANGITY CLANG
VIOLENS! A FIRE ALARM!
CLANGITY CLANGITY CLANG
UNH!
LOOKS LIKE YOU WERE RIGHT.
IT'S NOT OVER.
MISS SACHS? MISTER VIOLENS?
KATIE PULLED THE FIRE ALARM. I TOLD HER NOT TO.
YOU'RE A BIG LIAR!
AM NOT.
AM TOO.
I THINK THEY'RE DOIN' IT AGAIN.

NO, WE'RE NOT "DOIN' IT AGAIN," AND I DON'T CARE WHO PULLED THE ALARM.
WAIT OUTSIDE. COPS AND FIREMEN WILL BE HERE IN A MINUTE.
AND FOR CHRISSAKES, DON'T MENTION OUR NAMES TO ANYONE. GOT IT?
BE RIGHT BACK, ERNIE. JUST GETTING A SOUVENIR.
A SOUVENIR?! WHAT'RE YOU, NUTS?!
YEAH.
ABOUT YOU.
WHAT'S THAT THING?
MOLOCH WAS WEARING IT AROUND HIS NECK. CAME OFF IN THE FIGHT. I THINK I RECOGNIZE IT.
IT MIGHT LEAD US TO HIM... IF YOU'RE INTERESTED.
WELL, I VOTE YES. AND SO DOES GERRY THERE. HOW 'BOUT YOU, ERNIE?
AW, SCREW IT, CALL ME VIOLENS.
RAJAH

Sachs & VIOLENS™

KREWE OF J.J. & ERNIE

MARDI GRAS

George Pérez
John Stracuzzi

MADRE DE DIOS.
LIEUTENANT KELSO...WHAT'S GOING TO HAPPEN TO J.J. NOW?
WELL, WE'RE NOT SURE. OBVIOUSLY, WE WANT HER BACK IN NEW YORK.
BUT THE NEW ORLEANS D.A. WANTS HER TO STAY RIGHT HERE UNTIL THIS MARDI GRAS FIASCO IS SORTED OUT.
YOU'VE GOT ONE POPULAR SISTER, SISTER.
VIOLENTS
in THE STREETS

NOT TO MENTION THEY WANT TO GET THEIR HANDS ON HER ACCOMPLICE, ERNIE SCHULTZ.

I WANT TO THANK YOU FOR ALERTING ME, LIEUTENANT.
THESE THINGS YOU'VE TOLD ME 'NITA'S INVOLVED WITH... IT'S INSANITY.
WET FLOOR

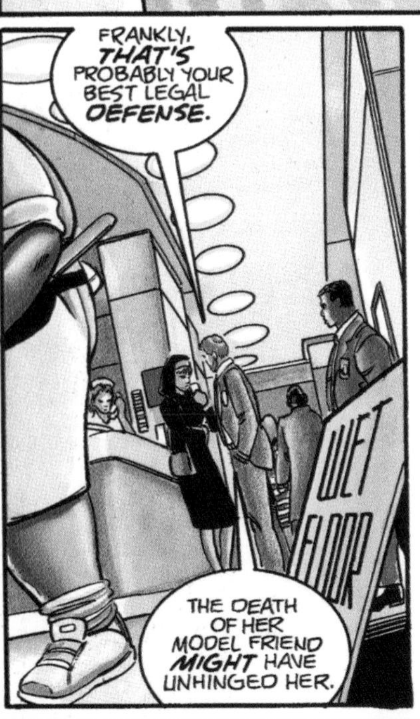
FRANKLY, THAT'S PROBABLY YOUR BEST LEGAL DEFENSE.
WET FLOOR
THE DEATH OF HER MODEL FRIEND MIGHT HAVE UNHINGED HER.

PLUS, WE THINK SCHULTZ WAS INFLUENCING HER. WITH HIS TRACK RECORD, HE WAS A TIME BOMB WAITING TO GO OFF.
STILL, SHE IS A SUSPECTED ACCOMPLICE IN 27 HOMICIDES BACK EAST...

NOT TO MENTION ALL THE SHIT WE'VE BEEN GETTING HERE, PARDON MY VULGARITY.
BE BEST FOR HER TO BE COMING CLEAN.

HAVE YOU SEEN
ALL RIGHT, GENTLEMEN, SHE'S AWAKE. BUT AT THE LEAST SIGN OF STRESS, YOU'RE GONE.

GET HER TO COOPERATE, SISTER. IT'S HER ONLY PRAYER.

M-Mac? Am I...back in New York?
NO, HON. I'VE COME TO LOUISIANA...
With a banjo on your knee?
Ohhh, God...Mac... I'm so SORRY...

Wanna know what HAPPENED?
NO.
SIS... TER...
SHE NEEDS A LAWYER.

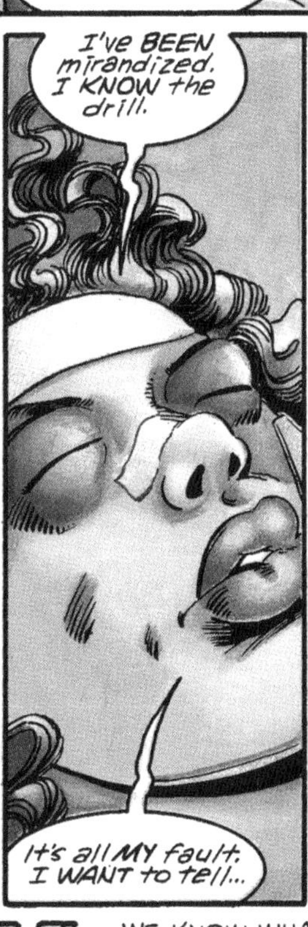
I've BEEN mirandized. I KNOW the drill.
It's all MY fault. I WANT to tell...

KEEP EVERY-BODY OUT...

NOW...YOU ACKNOWLEDGE YOU'RE MAKING THIS STATEMENT OF YOUR OWN FREE WILL?

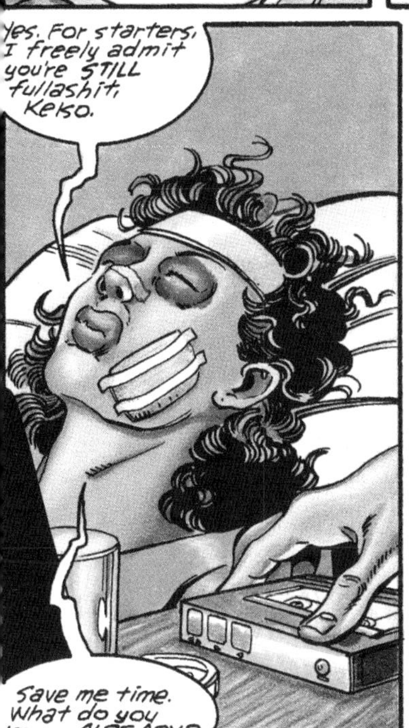
Yes. For starters, I freely admit you're STILL fullashit, Kelso.
Save me time. What do you know ALREADY?

WE KNOW WHAT HAPPENED IN NEW YORK. AND THE NEW JERSEY INCIDENT'S BEEN TRACED TO YOU, TOO.

'NITA, SAVING THESE CHILDREN WAS SO BRAVE... BUT IT WAS CRAZY. DO YOU SEE THAT?
New Orleans Hospital
It seemed... RIGHT... at the time.

We came to New Orleans chasing down the man who was running the children's ring.

Moloch. YOU remember. I asked you about that name.

It was a long drive, but we made it down there in REASONABLE time.

Miraculously, we managed to find a hotel room. Ernie zonked out...

And I finally had a chance to catch "NYPD Blue."

THAT'S IT?! THAT'S "DARING"? MILD PROFANITY AND SOME GUY'S BARE ASS?
WHAT'S "MATURE" ABOUT THAT? IT'S INFANTILE.

JEEZ, SOME "CREATORS" USE ANY EXCUSE TO TOSS IN GRATUITOUS NUDITY AND SWEAR WORDS. IT'S BULLSHIT.

UH OH.
NNN GGGG...

Once... around New Year's, I think, when Ernie was REALLY drunk... he told me about the DREAMS.
About the stuff that happened in Vietnam when he was a war photographer there.
He LAUGHED about it. He said... he said people didn't WORRY about 'Nam anymore. They'd moved on to AIDS and OTHER stuff.
He said that "disturbed Vietnam vets" were CLICHÉ. Then he laughed some more... and then he cried.

And he said something about... mothers and sons...and dying babies...stuff I DIDN'T understand...
Then he passed out. And when he came to, he PRETENDED he didn't remember he'd talked about it.
Maybe he DIDN'T.
VIOLETS
But we never discussed it again. Which is BETTER, I think.

YOU OKAY, ERNIE? YOU NEED TO SLEEP SOME MORE?
I'M FINE. BESIDES, WITH ALL THE RACKET OUT THERE, I'LL NEVER GET BACK TO SLEEP.
IT'S FAT TUESDAY, JJ, ON BOURBON STREET IN THE FRENCH QUARTER.
WELCOME TO THE FINAL DAY OF MARDI GRAS, THE WORLD'S WILDEST CELEBRATION. SHORT OF PEOPLE HURTING EACH OTHER, ANYTHING GOES.
BEADS FOR BUNS!!
I BEND OVER FOR BEADS!
KODAK

Show us what you got

I'LL TRADE SPAWN #1 FOR BEADS

HERE'S WHAT WE GOT, J.J. I TOOK THIS OFF MOLOCH IN OUR FIGHT.

IT'S A KREWE MEDALLION. KREWES ARE SOCIETIES THAT ORGANIZE PARADES AND SUCH FOR MARDI GRAS.
RAJAH
THE LEX AND KONO KREWES HAVE BEEN AROUND FOR DECADES.

BUT THE RAJAH KREWE WENT UNDER-GROUND, LATE 1800s...
WORD WAS THEY PRACTICED SATANIC RITUALS, SHIT LIKE THAT.
HOW DO YOU KNOW ALL THIS?

I USED TO LIVE AROUND HERE, BACK WHEN I WAS YOUNG AND ROBUST.

YOU'RE STILL ROBUST, ERNIE.

IN FACT...

C'MON!

RIGHT HERE.
RIGHT NOW.
YOU'RE KIDDING.

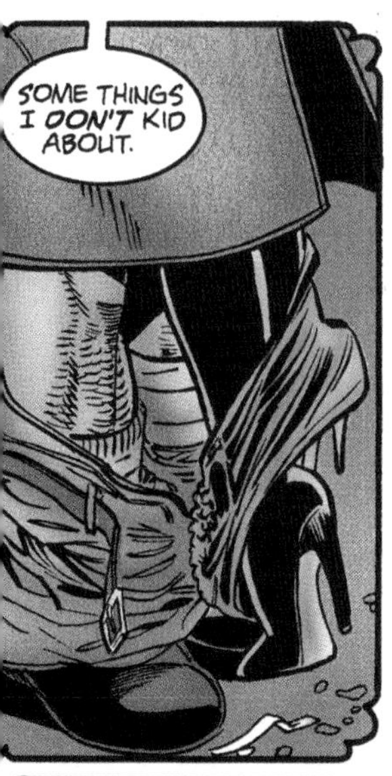
SOME THINGS I DON'T KID ABOUT.

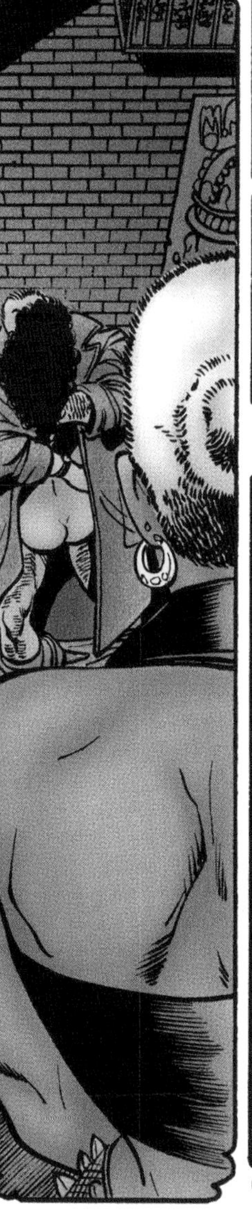

WHAT DO YOU FIND SO INTRIGUING, MY SWEET RUG-MUNCHER?
NOTHING. SAME SHIT, DIFFERENT DAY.

THERE'S NO DAY MORE DIFFERENT THAN THIS.

COME, MY DEAR. WE HAVE PLACES TO GO.

REST OF THE NIGHT'S GONNA BE DOWN-HILL.

THE RAJAH'S HISTORIC MEETING PLACE WAS RUMORED TO BE A BUILDING AROUND THIS...
...CORNER?

YOU WILL BURN IN HELL! REPENT BEFORE IT'S TOO LATE!
LEFT RIGHT CENTRIST headquarters
YOU'LL ALL BURN IN HELL!!
SATANISTS? IN THAT BUILDING THERE?
YEAH.
REPENT
THINGS CHANGE, HUH?

MEBBE. OR MAYBE THEY JUST CLEAN UP THEIR ACT.
WAIT HERE.

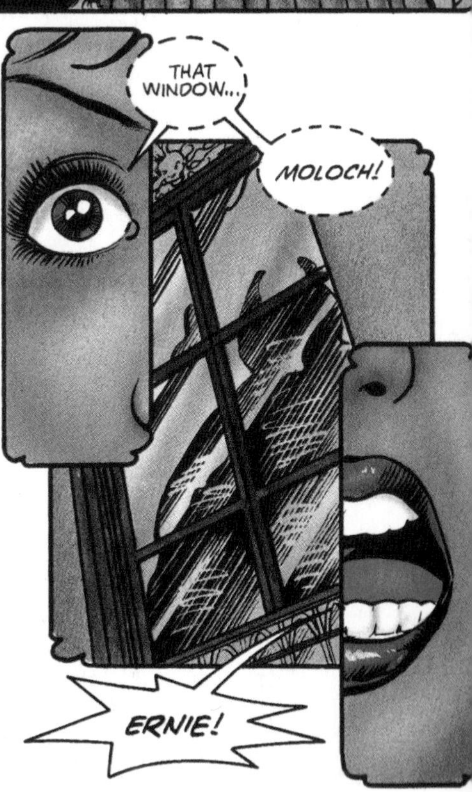
THAT WINDOW...
MOLOCH!
ERNIE!

YOU GUYS ARE DEAD-ON. THIS CELEBRATION OF DEPRAVITY...
BUT WHAT CAN ANYONE DO ABOUT IT?
REPENT BEFORE IT'S TOO LATE!
YOU'D BE AMAZED. I MEAN, WITH BUSH AND QUAYLE REPLACED BY AN ADULTEROUS POT SMOKER, YOU CAN FORGET ABOUT MORALITY FROM ON HIGH.
WE, THE PEOPLE, ARE GONNA SHOW EVERYONE.
JUST WAIT. YOU'LL SEE...

UH, CHONG... HOW'S ABOUT IF YOU SHUT THE HELL UP?
TODDLE ON HOME, GRAMPS.

PEACE, GUYS. MY GENERATION PRACTICALLY INVENTED PROTESTS.
ALONG WITH DRUGS AND PROMISCUITY. KEEP MOVING.

LITTLE PRICK.
J.J.! THINK A RELIGIOUS ORGANIZATION WOULD BE A GOOD COVER FOR THE RAJAH?

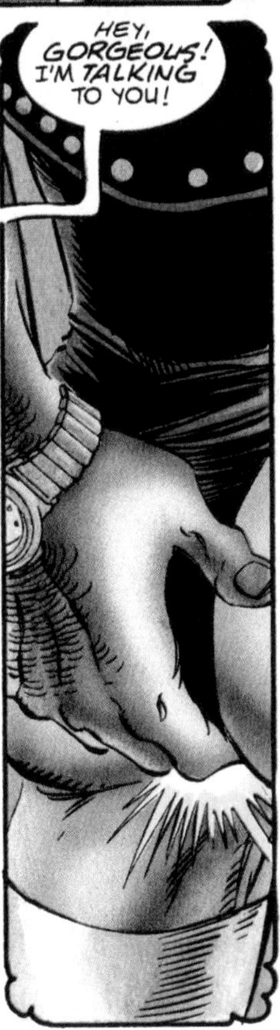
HEY, GORGEOUS! I'M TALKING TO YOU!

I'M ALL EARS. MY NAME'S LEO.
OY. I'M SORRY.

I'M NOT. I ADORE BORGNINE-TYPES.
J.J.! WHERE ARE YOU?!

LEFT
RIGHT
CENTRIST
headquarters
YOU'RE DAMNED LUCKY YOU'RE MY BROTHER, MOLOCH. AFTER YOUR LETTING THE CHILD RING GET SMASHED...
I CAN ALWAYS REBUILT IT, BIG O. BESIDES, WHY HARP ON ONE FAILURE?
WHO SET UP THE CENTRISTS, AFTER ALL?
I'LL GRANT YOU THAT. HISTORY SAYS THAT, FOR MAXIMUM IMPACT, GO WITH RELIGIOUS FANATICS.
THEY'LL DESTROY ANYTHING IF IT'S IN GOD'S NAME.

HEN AGAIN, OURS IS A DIVERSIFIED ORGANIZATION ATERING TO PERVERSION ON ONE HAND AND STRIK-ING OUT AT OVERT SEXUAL-TY ON THE OTHER.
MIXED MESSAGES ARE THE BEST. MAKES THE FORBIDDEN FRUIT THAT MUCH SWEETER.
SO THE DEVICE IS HERE, YOU SAY? BY THE WHEELBASE?
EXCELLENT PLACEMENT. YOUR PEOPLE DO GOOD WOR--
WHOA AAAH!
WHAT WAS THAT?!
I DON'T KNOW! CHECK IT OUT!
YOU SAYING "CHECK IT OUT" SOUNDS LIKE THE OLD DAYS...
SHUT UP AND DO IT!
WELL, WELL! I WAS SPYING YOU WITH MY LITTLE EYE EARLIER, FROM BIG O'S BALCONY...BOFFING SOME GUY IN A COAT...
OHHHH, MEROE. YOU'RE HER, AREN'T YOU?... THE LEATHER LADY FROM UP EAST.
COME HERE, SCRUMPTIOUS.

COME TO
RUGMUNCHER.

AHHHHH!!!

OOOOF!

GET HER! GET THAT CRAZY BITCH!

ERNIE! THANK GOD!

WE GOT A BIG PROBLEM! C'MON!

OUTTA THE WAY!

ERNIE! QUO VADIS? DIFFICULTIES?
STAY OUTTA THIS, LEO.
WHERE D'YOU KNOW HIM FROM?!
LATER! NOW TELL ME THE "BIG PROB-LEM."
SHE'S GOT THE FAT SLOB WITH HER! MOVE!
WELL!
WHOA!
DAMN!
I DID WHAT I COULD, ERNIE BORGNINE.
ADIEU, MON COEUR.

SO THAT'S THE STORY! WE GOTTA FIND THE BOMB IN THE PARADE FLOAT AND--!
NO! ENOUGH, J.J.! ENOUGH! I CAN'T PLAY ALONG WITH THIS ANYMORE!

RISKING OUR NECKS IS ONE THING, BUT THERE'S A MILLION PEOPLE HERE!

WE TELL THE COPS! RIGHT NOW!

HOW DO WE SAY WE FOUND OUT?
WE SAY WE OVERHEARD. IT'S THE TRUTH, AIN'T IT?

UH-OH.

ERNIE, I KNOW THAT GUY! HE'S FROM NEW YORK!

NEXT TIME YOU'RE ON THE RUN, DON'T USE TRACEABLE CREDIT CARDS AT A HOTEL.
No choice! Low on CASH.
ONCE I KNEW YOU WERE HERE, I TOOK SOME VACATION TIME AND SHOT DOWN HERE.
WHY?

YOU KIDDING? THIS CASE IS SENSATIONAL! GUNS, WHIPS, LEATHER, MASS MURDER, CHAOS. WE'RE TALKING HOLLYWOOD, TV MOVIES, BOOK AND COMIC BOOK DEALS. THE WORKS.

YOU WANT TO MAKE MONEY OFF THIS?!
SAVE THE "HOLIER-THAN-THOU" STUFF.

I GOT FOUR DAUGHTERS TO PUT THROUGH COLLEGE AND MARRY OFF AND I'M NOT ON THE PAD.
SO I NEED ALL THE HELP I CAN GET.

WE coulda' used some help.
But NOOO. All we got was--

THAT'S HER! ARREST HER! AND HIM!!!
RYAN! SIMONS! THE BIG GUY AND THE LEATHER BROAD! GET 'EM!

GREAT!
NOW WHAT ?!

I DUNNO! YOU'RE THE BRAINS HERE!
SINCE WHEN?!
SINCE NOW!

OKAY! WE CLEAR THE STREETS, FIND THE FLOAT, AND DISARM THE BOMB!
EASY!
EXCEPT FOR THAT WE'RE PACKED IN LIKE SARDINES, THERE'S A THOUSAND FLOATS, AND I KNOW JACK SHIT ABOUT DISARMING BOMBS, THAT'S A GREAT PLAN!
MOVE! ALL OF YOU! SCRAM!
WHAT'RE YOU, NUTS?!?
THAT'S WHAT MY PAROLE OFFICER KEEPS ASKING! NOW GET OUTTA HERE!
VIOLENS! I SEE IT! DOWN THE END OF THE STREET!
THE MAIN LEX FLOAT? YOU SURE?

POSITIVE!
STOP THOSE LUNATICS!
THEY'RE RUINING THE PARADE!

YOU IDIOTS! WE'RE TRYING TO SA--
AW, SCREW IT.
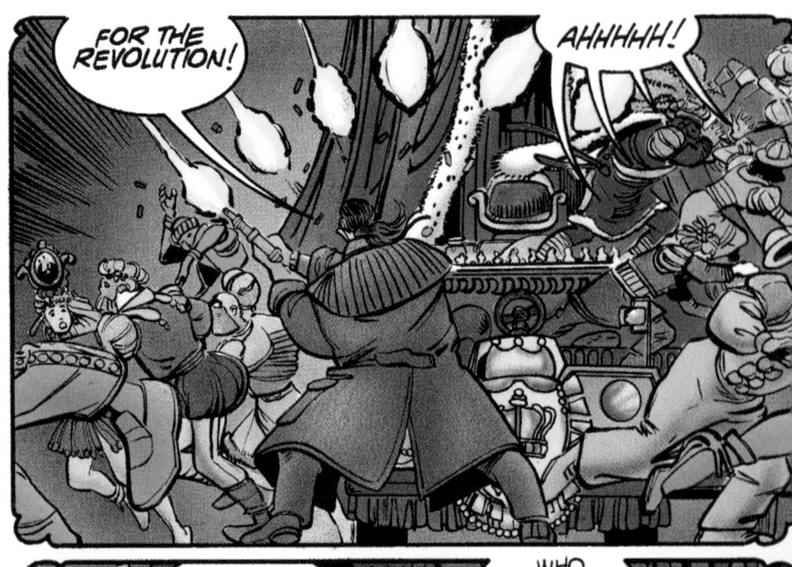
FOR THE REVOLUTION!
AHHHHH!

WHAT REVOLUTION?
WHO KNOWS? IT SOUNDED TERRORIST-LIKE.

3:24
3:23
AWWW, SHIT.

WELL, WE EITHER GOT THREE HOURS OR THREE MINUTES.
ME, I'M GUESSING MINUTES.
PULL THE BOMB OUT!

TOO WIRED UP. IF I DO, IT'LL BLOW EARLY.
KEEP GOING. LOSE YOURSELF IN THE CROWD.
ERNIE! WHAT'RE YOU DOING?!?

I LOVE YOU, J.J.
YOU'RE THE DEMENTED WACKO OF MY DREAMS.
OWWW!
NOW GET LOST.

Ernie wasn't trying to HURT anybody. He was trying to SAVE everybody.

He is... he WAS... a hero.

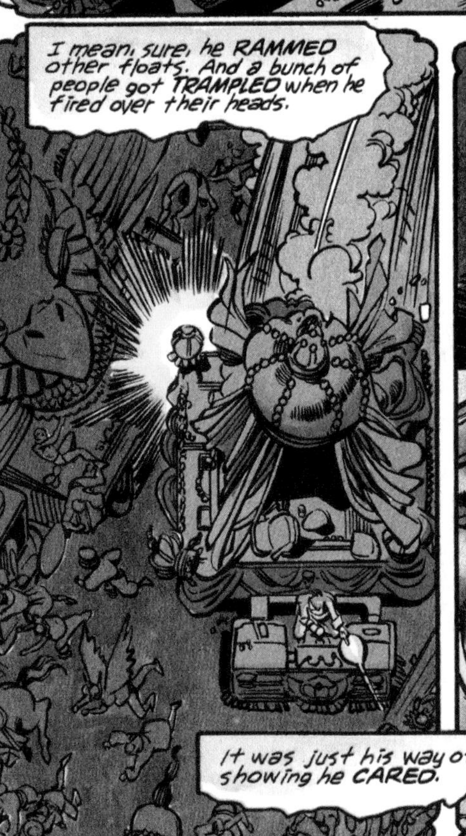
I mean, sure, he RAMMED other floats. And a bunch of people got TRAMPLED when he fired over their heads.
It was just his way of showing he CARED.

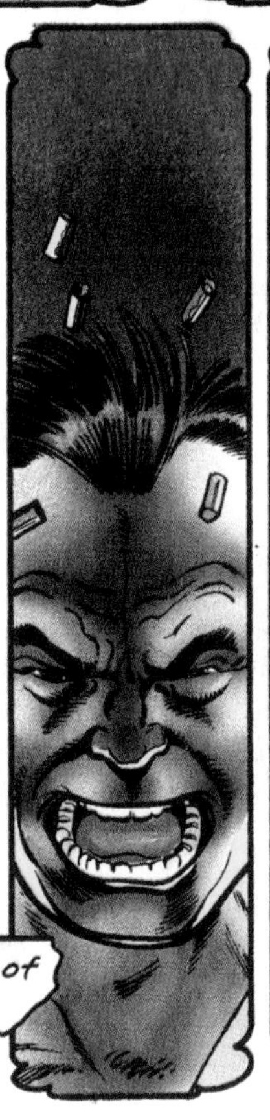

OWW!
YOU AGAIN!
YOU KNOW, CHERIE, I'VE ONLY KNOWN YOU FOR A FEW MINUTES...
...AND ALREADY I CAN'T STAND YOU.
KIND OF A SHAME, REALLY.
ACKKK!
YOU, ME, AND BIG O...
WE COULD'VE HAD FUN TOGETHER.
VIOLENS !!!
SACHS --?!

SACHS! YOU LUNATIC! I KNOCKED YOU CLEAR! WHAT'RE YOU PLAYING AT?!
YOU'RE A DETERMINED ONE, AREN'T YOU?
WON'T ABANDON YOUR PARTNER, NO MATTER WHAT I CAN RESPECT THAT.
LET'S GO, SWEETHEART. NO NEED FOR YOUR SCRUMPTIOUS BODY TO TAKE THIS KIND OF ABUSE.

HEY, RUGMUNCHER!

MUNCH THIS.

BUDDA
BUDDA
BUDDA
BUDDA

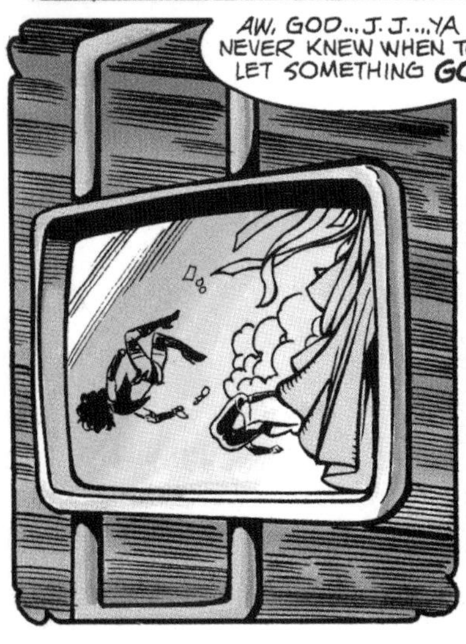

AW, GOD... J. J. ...YA NEVER KNEW WHEN TO LET SOMETHING GO.

OVER THERE! PERFECT!
EXCEPT... TIME'S ALMOST UP! NOT GONNA MAKE IT! SHI--

IT WAS ALL *MY FAULT!* UNDER-STAND, KELSO, YOU DUMB *SHIT?* HE DID IT ALL FOR *ME!*

ERNIE'S PROBABLY *DEAD* NOW! AND IF HE *DID* MANAGE TO LEAP CLEAR, THEN JUST... JUST LEAVE HIM *ALONE*. THE HELL *ALONE!* YOU--

WE'RE *DONE*, DETECTIVE. I'M *ORDERING* YOU TO LEAVE.

'S'FINE. WE'RE *FINISHED* HERE.

YOU *COMING*, SISTER?

Mac... stay. PLEASE ...?
SURE. YOU BET.

YOU BE KEEPING YOUR EYES OPEN.
YES SIR.

I DON'T KNOW WHO TO CALL FIRST: THE D.A. OR "HARD COPY."
CAUTION WET FLOOR

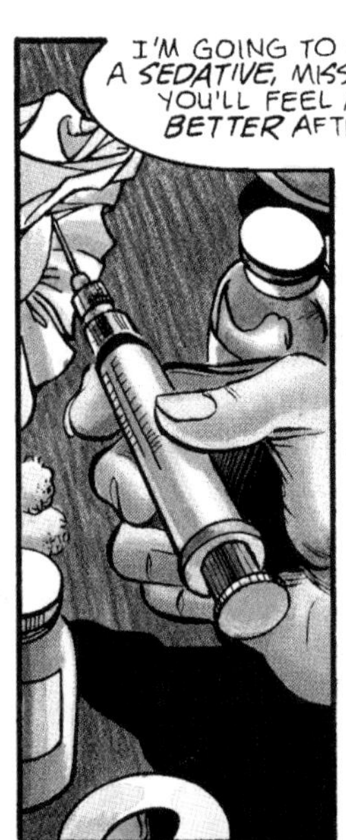
I'M GOING TO PREPARE A SEDATIVE, MISS SACHS. YOU'LL FEEL MUCH BETTER AFTER...

EXCUSE ME! NO MOPPING JUST NOW, IF YOU DON'T MIND.

DON'T MIND A BIT.

MOLOCH! IT'S MOLOCH!
SHE'S GETTING DELIRIOUS!

NO.
SHE'S GETTING DEAD.

SHE AND THE DEAD COP OUTSIDE...
...CAN COMPARE NOTES...

...IN HELL.

HEEEE-YAAHHH!
OOOH! NICE FORM! YOU'RE OUTTA PRACTICE, THOUGH.

HAIL MARY, FULL OF GRACE.
PUNCH A NUN RIGHT IN THE FACE.
UNHHH!!!

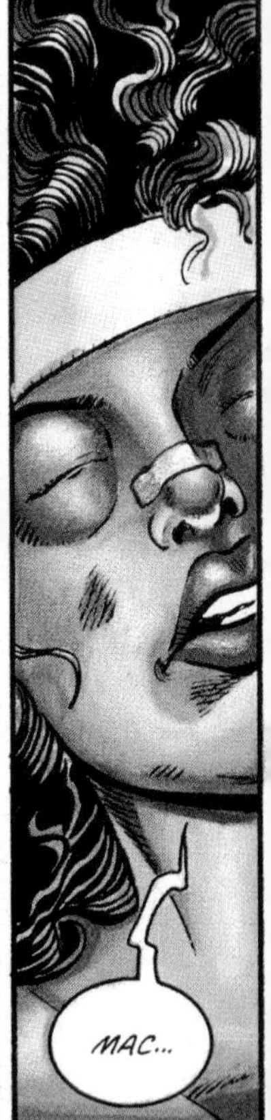
MAC...

DON'T HURT ME! I'M...I'M...I'M GETTING MARRIED NEXT WEEK!
WANNA BET?

GET AWAY! GET AWAY FROM HER!
OOOFF!

GEEZ, AND I THOUGHT THE NUNS BACK IN CATHOLIC SCHOOL WERE A PAIN!
OKAY, SISTER! YOU WANNA DIE FIRST? YOU GOT IT!

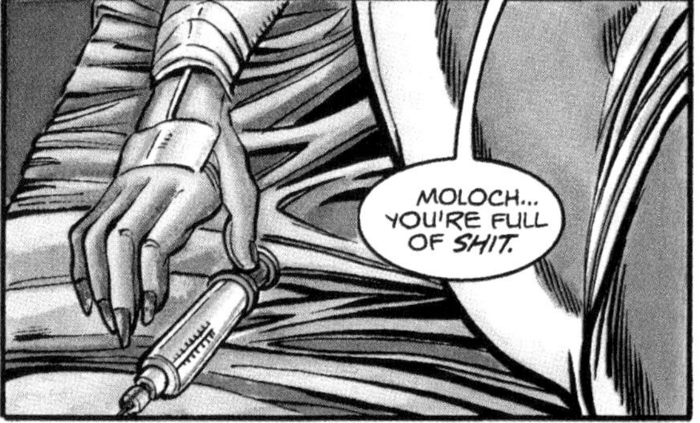
MOLOCH... YOU'RE FULL OF SHIT.

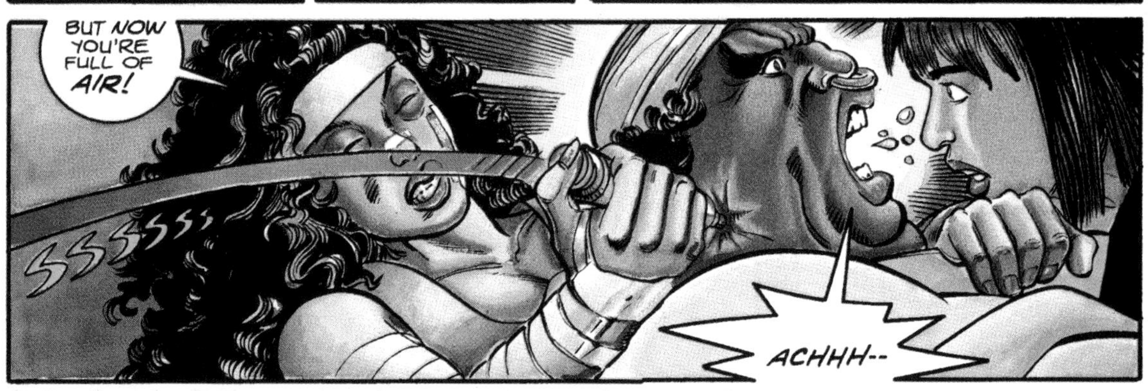
BUT NOW YOU'RE FULL OF AIR!
SSSSSSS
ACHHH--

NOW WHAT ?!?

MISTER TIMING.
WHAT HAPPENED ?!
THIS IS MAC, BY THE WAY.
I READ IF YOU GET AN AIRBUBBLE IN YOUR BLOOD, YOU DIE. GUESS SO.
UH... HI. A PLEASURE.
AW, SHIT!
FREEZE!
MISTER TIMING.
IT WAS HIM, WASN'T HIM?
YES. HE CAME BACK FOR HER... THOUGH THEY LEFT YOU MOLOCH.
ERNIE SAID THEY HAVE TO BE LIKE SHARKS NOW. KEEP MOVING OR DIE.
DAMN. DAMN!
CHEER UP, LIEUTENANT! THE BETTER FOR YOU, RIGHT?
AS LONG AS THEY'RE ON THE RUN...
...YOU CAN MILK MORE BLOOD MONEY OUT OF THE STORY...
...OF SACHS AND VIOLENS.